Author's name:Καλλιόπη Καπλανίδου- Kalliopi Kaplanidou

ISBN: 978-618-85784-5-6

For more information about the author: https://amazingcreationsshop.wixsite.com/kalliopisstories/about-in-greek

How to set goals and succeed by improving your daily habits!

Prologue.

In these pages that you are about to read you will learn how to set goals correctly for all areas of your life and how to achieve them. You won't find magic solutions. You will need to take the time and put into practice what you will read. No one can do it for you! **Your happiness is in your hand! You deserve a better and more quality life in all areas of your life.** What are you waiting for? Will you react differently this time and will you commit to taking action and following all the steps that will be given to you on the following pages or will you simply read them and continue to do the same?

The decision is yours!

****

How I ended up with all this information that I'm going to share with you:

Like so many others, as soon as the new year came, I decided to set my new goals. The difference with my previous times was that for 2 years I attended various free seminars on this topic. Due to the pandemic, many notable people held free seminars on various topics.

I searched and found my old notes from various books I've read in the last 10 years and I'm sorry to say that but I don't remember titles and authors after so many years that have passed (I have this with names, titles, dates) to tell you which it was. I don't keep the books I read because of lack of space and because I feel better about myself if I give every book, I read to the library so that someone else who might not be able to afford it can read it (as I once was).

You will certainly save time searching and finding all this information that I will share with you because I did it for you.

****

At the end of this book, I will give you the links and the names of the free seminars from which I gained so much knowledge and some of which I share with you, and various other sources that are equally useful. Sign up so that when they do a free seminar again, you can participate! They are worthy don't miss them! Most of them are in English and you will need to know English to watch them.

****

I hope the time you will spend reading these pages will not be wasted and, in the end, you will feel that you really got something useful! I hope and wish that something from what you will read will help you get activated, and inspired and start taking action in a way that will improve your life!

****

I will write them in the form of notes. Something can be said again in a different way. I will leave it for the purpose of touching someone who perhaps the first way was not so clear to him but the second way that is written help him understand it better. Don't worry you're not going to read a few basic things that will be repeated over and over again. No. Some will simply exist with different examples and in a different way because they will be an extension of some other techniques.

Let's start!

****

Check your inner circle:
Do you have at least one negative person in your life?
When you talk about your dreams your goals to this person, do you have to hold back your excitement because they will start talking in a way that will cut your feathers or make fun of you? So, you end up talking in a less enthusiastic way to protect yourself from them?
Example:
You're forced to say: I know you're right…. We are living in hard times but I don't know….I think I may try it just to get it off my mind.
Instead of saying "I have decided and I will…!"
This is a very bad habit, which our mind listens to, it listens to these miserable ways we talk about our goals. And think that we don't want to have what we describe when we talk in such a way.

God gave you this goal! Why do you want others to accept your goals so you can speak about them with love and determination? Why is this so important to you? Think about it! Go deeper and write the why. You have to discover what label/belief is limiting you before you can banish it forever.

The goal is yours, not theirs, so don't expect them to be proud of you for having that goal. They have other wants and think differently than you so how do you expect them to understand you and agree with you?

Do it, go ahead, act, and don't talk about your goal to such people, don't wait for them to like your ideas first before you can act on them!
****

To change your life, you have to change the way you see the problems that come into your life!

The bigger a problem is it means an even bigger success is coming. Don't be afraid of problems but welcome them with joy and say "something better is coming into my life, a great opportunity!"
The storm when it comes never lasts forever!
So don't give up!
Yeah, okay, you're right, the new problem scared you and your old habits jumped out on you so now you're starting to say things like 'why me? Not again, why God hates me so much…blah blah blah"
But consider the following:

If the world ended today, would you care at all about this problem? Or would you say I don't give a…. and went on thinking how to enjoy your last day on earth?
It's enough, don't cry anymore about what happened to you, but find a solution to it!
Did this habit of overreacting (in a negative way) every time a difficulty came up help you?
Has this habit of exaggerating the problem in your mind helped you?
Has this habit of staying stuck on the idea that you have to deal with a problem and then just hanging on to the fact that you got that difficulty helped you in the past rather than focusing on how you're going to solve it?
Why not train yourself to react differently!
There's trouble coming, say **THAT'S FINE**!
Say out loud **WHAT A JOY! I'm ready for it! I was born ready to solve every problem that comes to me!**
Jump up and down like a child full of joy who just got the toy he always wanted!
Yes, think of a happy moment and think about it strongly and react strongly, feel it even happier than it was! Even if you have to force yourself to feel and think something beautiful, do it and live it as happily as you can. **This way you stop the panic you were feeling and you are focusing on something positive. This way it will be easy for you to think more wisely and deal with the solution as well.**

Every time you catch yourself exaggerating the problem, think of a pleasant moment and magnify it!
Stop this bad habit of exaggerating and scaring without solving the problem! Say out loud "***whatever happens I will find the solution***!"
Then ask yourself this question: **If the world ended today, would I care? Would this problem really scare me so much?**
This question helps you calm down and see that the problem is not so tragic after all. But don't forget to ask and answer that question!
Stop yourself every time you find yourself overreacting to the problem, don't let it become huge in your mind!
It's not that huge!
Think about this too, can you find solutions if you are in a state of panic and despair?

Go and find a group of people who learn how to set goals, and how to think positively and why not ask them to help you see the positive in your problem. Because of your panic, you are failing to see it! By doing so, you don't react like before. You are starting a new better habit. You take new reaction steps that are more practical that will help you find solutions!

Problems mean opportunities for growth and new doors are waiting for you to open them. I know what you're going to say "yeah right, you're safe outside of the problem and suggesting all these things to me, but come "wear my shoes" and then tell me all these things".

I can't put myself in your shoes (but I may have been in your shoes), but don't forget that you're the one looking for tips on how to change the way you react to the problems that come your way. Therefore, you are given a piece of advice. Why not try it?
Try it again and again! Make them your new habit.

I also suggest watching the videos of **Dean Graziosi και Tony Robbins** to cheer you up and maybe help you on finding solutions! Their vitality is incredible! They will supply you - they will fill you with enthusiasm and appetite to act! The free seminars they did were a godsend! Some of the information you will read is also from their free seminars. Also, at the end of the book, you will find some online groups to try communicating with people who are learning like you how to improve their lives.
****

I take all the responsibility on me!

When something goes wrong the first thing, we do is to think about who is to blame. Where do we lay the blame? "Surely it's someone else's fault and not mine."
This way of thinking will prevent you from learning the life lesson that this difficulty wants to teach you.
It will prevent you from seeing what you did wrong and so the problem will not go away as quickly and as painlessly as possible. But it will continue to exist and you will continue to suffer.
This way of thinking will prevent you from seeing any solutions that exist and any opportunities that arise because of this difficulty that appeared! This will result in you being stuck in the problem angry, filled with a bunch of negative emotions waiting for someone to save you instead of trying to find a solution and help yourself.

A wiser way of looking at the whole situation is this:
No one will save me because I will save myself! No one else is to blame and I will not blame anyone else. I will not waste my precious time blaming others! I won't get caught up in thinking about who was at fault and why. I will not be filled with anger and many other negative emotions!
My time is precious!
Now is my chance to succeed!

By solving the problem, I will not only become a stronger person but I will discover new ways to succeed in my life!
I will find new ways to improve the quality of my life!

But in order to be able to think positively and dynamically in this way, you must first calm down and stop feeling panic and anger. You have to focus on finding solutions and implementing the solution! Ask again the question we've asked above about how important and terrifying your problem would be if you knew the world was coming to an end and we were all going to die today.

Say it out loud:
I count on me!
What I need now is in me!
I have achieved so much in my life!
I am where I am because I thought about what I needed in every moment of my life and took the steps I needed (to learn things, to study, to act, to overcome) and that's what I've been doing for so many years! So, I can do that now too!
I can shine and end up learning huge life lessons and opening new doors full of opportunities to shine once again!
I'm all set! Bring it up!
And if you have a lot of complaints about the way the world is today, about the economy and world politics, first fix the problems inside your house, then improve yourself, build your income and you will see that the outside world will also start to look better and full of opportunities.
Don't just stop on the complaints! Act! Start to positively improve your life and help others!

****

Who gives you advice?

Do you feel like you are not in control of your life?
Do you feel like you've been doing what other people told you all your life?
Change it!
Who gives you advice?
Do they have the necessary experience or expertise on the problem or goal you are asking them for advice on?
Are you consulting the wrong person?
I'll give you an example of what I mean when I say the wrong person. Are you looking for advice on how to find a job or how to increase your income from someone who is unemployed or has failed in this field?

Change that habit of asking the wrong people for advice and learn what you need from people who have succeeded at what you want to learn to do well.

Get advice from people who have made it.

Watch their videos, read their books, and pay them to show you how they did it and what you need to do.

Because the advice you will get from people who have succeeded will be your sure guide to success.

Don't be filled with fear because someone tells you that you should be afraid because what you want to do is impossible or too difficult.

Don't fill your mind with negative thoughts, negative news, negative people, and negative advice.

Do things that fill you with vitality! That motivates you! That excites you!

Ask yourself: (Take a pen and paper and write your answers to the following questions.)

1. What am I doing and seeing that makes me feel like I'm not leading my life? Think about this for a bit!
2. What are those things you keep doing, keep watching, and keep hearing that keep you from shining / succeeding your goals?
3. Do you watch a lot of TV?
4. Do you spend hours on Facebook or any of the social media?
5. Are you negatively affected by what?
6. What do you use up your energy and after you are very tired and you end up not doing what will lead you to where you want to be?

Stop it! Stop filling yourself with negativity!

Stop wasting your time on pointless things that only offer you fatigue which will not allow you to deal with what you want and what leads you to a better quality of life, with more freedom.

Change what you do and do things that make you feel alive and optimistic!

****

I will start my day with love.

Love your customers, love what you do, love the work you do and everything else you do.

Why;

Because you should love giving to others!

Make the customers love the business owner or the employee that is you!

Have excellent service.

Have excellent communication with customers.

Have excellent communication with everyone you work with!

Love your product or your work!
Love what you do no matter what!

If you are an employee and you do all of the above, you might even get a promotion, because what boss wants to lose an employee who is so valuable?
Or a partner or client could suggest to you to go and work with them with better conditions!

 No matter what, you will feel less dissatisfaction with such a mindset! **And the hours will be more pleasant and less charged with anger and frustration when you do things that are difficult or their circumstances are difficult!**
****

Be brave!

Don't let fear stop you!
Do it even if you are afraid or uncomfortable because it is something new for you.
Don't let boredom stop you! Don't allow negative people to influence you and stop you!
Don't wait for the perfect / right time to come, it will never come because the perfect time is **now**!
Don't wait for everything to be perfect, **do it now**!
 Don't hesitate waiting for your friends and family to like your idea or waiting for when and if they will approve it, **do it now**!
****

Focus on the solution.

Train your mind to think:
What can I learn from this situation?
What is the solution?

Instead of starting to think "now what will I do, what will I become?" and dwelling only on these kinds of thoughts, filling your mind with a bunch of negative scenarios and negative emotions (anger, frustration, etc.), **accept the situation and focus only on the solution!**
Make the problem, the setback and the difficulty go away faster by finding the solutions!
Free your mind from worrying about the problem and think about solutions and how you will come out victorious from all this!
Search to see how others have solved similar problems!
Google may have the answers! You never know! Search! Activate yourself positively!

The problem is here now so focus on finding the solution (Start solving it) and not only that! See the opportunities that appear!

****

Pay attention to the little everyday things!

There are small daily habits that you can incorporate into your daily life that have the potential to take you to the next level. Don't start giving the classic excuses "I don't have free time I'm running around all day... I'll forget to take the positive steps …. I will never escape the way I live...etc." There is a solution!

Set alarms to remind you to use "the positive way of thinking»!

If you really want to succeed and get out of your misery you will!

Put stickers on the most popular places in your house with positive thinking words and your goals!

At first, when we get out of our routine, everything seems difficult and boring.

It's easier to just complain than to make small changes in our daily life to have a better-quality life.

Set alarms saying -to your cell phone- during the day as a reminder:

"I take responsibility, no one is to blame!"

«Instead of getting angry and resentful, I will act with love! ».

«Not to forget to watch or listen to something for at least half an hour that will make me laugh! ».

"Remember to focus on the solution and not on the problem and not getting angry!"

«You deserve it, my girl, you deserve it!" etc.

Notice how you feel and as soon as you realize that a negative emotion has arisen, don't let it exist for a long time! Do something that will reduce the intensity of the negative emotion and why not banish it completely!

Have a funny video ready or a specific YouTube channel that always makes you laugh or motivates/inspires you.

Always have with you the paper on which you have written your goals and the paper with your positive statements (put them on your mobile phone so that if the mobile phone battery is full, you can see them from there, otherwise have the paper with you) and instead of getting upset because you're waiting in a long line or because you're in traffic moving so slow read or listen to them. **Change your mood**!

Listen to your favorite music or a program for self-improve while you wait!

Before you go home, unwind by watching a sunset or by going for a walk in nature or by going for a walk in general, or by suggesting to a friend or your partner to go for a walk or go exercise in some way. **Find a way to laugh a lot!**

Always have ready the tools with which you will reduce the intensity of your negative emotions and keep your attention on your goals and the positives of the day!

****

I will persist until I succeed!

Don't give up because you might be one step away from success. **You don't know how close you are to your success so don't give up**!
No matter how difficult your day was, repeat this to yourself many times:
 «**I won't give up! I won't stop!
My success is very close so I will not stop now!**"
Focus on your goal!

Every time you want to give up, start thinking about your goal and the freedom it will give you when you will have it! Instead of thinking negatively, picture it in your mind that you are reaching your goal and you are enjoying your new life! Imagine it with as much detail as you can on what your new life is like now that you've made it!
Keep your focus away from "I want to give up" to "I made it! I enjoy a life full of quality, freedom, etc.».
Strengthen with emotion and positivity and the will to achieve your goal in your mind and get into a new mindset to think positively and do what we said above! Practice on all of them **NOW**!

****

Who and How.

We set a goal or want something, to implement an idea.
Our mind comes and asks us "It is fine to want but how will you put it into practice?
How will you do it?
How will you start?
Are you capable of doing it?
Do you have everything you need to do it?"
If not then look at the environment around you.
Has anyone done this successfully so you can ask for advice and help?

He may be an acquaintance of yours or simply a professional in this kind of thing, who lives in your city or whom you have heard of. You can ask him to teach you, advise you (even work for free a few hours next to him every week) he may say no but he may also say yes. Follow his steps (His interviews. If he has published a book buy it. If he has videos on some platform go watch them. If he does courses pay and learn from him).

If you don't know how to do it pay someone who knows how to do it to do it for you. Start classes to gain the skills you need that you don't have. Even online courses. If you don't know someone look it up online, find people who have done it, and learn from them!
 Instead of getting stuck thinking how hard it is because you don't have the skills or don't even know how to do it take the above steps and try them.

Change this habit of always seeing only obstacles and excuses not to act, only dwelling on the idea and then giving up.
You have the internet that can help you search and find out how others are doing it!
Well, what are you waiting for, go ahead!
Start your own research or pay someone to do it for you!
Act on your idea, your goal!
Act!!
Break your goal down into small steps to better understand what you need to do and what skills you don't have and what skills you need to have and why not pay someone who has the skills you don't have or build a team of people to fill your gaps.
Write down your goal on paper or your computer and break down all the basic steps needed. What other steps need to be taken? As you progress, you will write which ones you did, which ones worked and which ones didn't, and what new things are needed, etc. This way you will remember everything you did, what you need to do, etc. Put this plan somewhere visible and look at it often during the day so you don't forget what your goal is and track its progress!

Don't drown in the idea that it's something huge and how you're going to succeed. Break it down into small steps and see what you're missing and how to fill your gaps! Don't get stuck on "I'm too old for these things…., I don't know how…., how can I learn all these things that need…….". You can do it!

There are so many others out there with the skills you need, but with no ideas! You have the ideas! Connect with them, work with them!
****
How to set goals effectively

Instead of the classic move, we make when the year changes or just before it changes (we simply set new goals and then forget about them) let's try to do something else and establish it every year!
Answer the following questions and work with the steps given to you!

1. What have you done wrong in the last 12 months?

What do you regret?
What did you try and it didn't work?
What did you say you were going to do and haven't even started?
What did you start and never finish?
In which field are you saying, *I tried it but*.... even if you didn't try everything but still you keep saying "***but I tried everything it wasn't possible...***"?
What was it that you didn't do on purpose because you were embarrassed or felt like you'd fail if you did?
How does it make you feel that you didn't do everything you wanted to do in the past year?

A) Think of relationships that have broken up in these 12 months...what did you learn from them?
How did being away from these people change you?
How did it help you?
Did you learn yourself better?
Did you learn better what your weaknesses are?
Did you learn a little better what not to do again or what to do next time in a similar situation?

What do you learn by answering all of the above?
Too many!
You will realize what went wrong and you remain stagnant.
What are your weaknesses, what did you do wrong.
How are you sabotaging your success.

All those exercises will help you know what complaints you have about yourself and life. It will help you better understand how you think, how negatively you think, what you need to correct, reinforce it with a positive way of thinking and a positive way of reacting, and much more.
You set some goals. But when a few weeks passed you reacted in the same way again (you lost your enthusiasm, you gave them up). This has to change.
You deserve a better quality of life why not have it?

B) Look at it another way. Now that you have written the above and can see them whenever you need, let's move on. Another year passed without doing what you wanted and what you said you would do in the time that passed. What happened, happened! Let them be! That's behind you now!

Forget how much you regret or how disappointed you felt that you didn't do what you wanted, that you didn't get where you wanted, and let time pass for one more year.
You are where you are and **no one can stop you from starting now with passion**!

Take with you only what gives you the passion you need to do what you want and forget what fills you with negative emotions.

Think that what you didn't do was because it wasn't the time to do it and stop blaming yourself.

Say, **"I wasn't ready, what happen - happen!" What I wanted was not ready to come to me! But now it is!........"** take only the lessons that all this taught you and keep only those that give you the strength to move forward with passion!
2. Let's continue!
Make a list of what went well in the past 12 months!
What did you start?
What did you do? (What steps did you take on the goals / ideas you said you would do 12 months ago, even if new better ideas came to you, what were they?)
What did you achieve (the small successes that you had even those daily small successes like not getting angry like before, walking 3 times a week etc. in the past year but also the big ones)?
Even in what you haven't finished yet, **feel great! You have started them!** You got out of your comfort zone and act on them! **You did not let them go without acting on them! Every small victory will lead you to a bigger victory and fill you with the passion to keep going!** That's why it's so important to keep a record (write them down) of what you've started and your small victories! _We tend to forget them and think only of failures and what we didn't do and this is a very negative self-destructive wrong mechanism that sabotages us_! **Write them to give you strength! Just think about what you started and did and nothing else!**
You want to find the strength and courage to continue so think only these kinds of things and feel incredible joy!!!!!!
We only think about what we didn't do and what went wrong!
Learn to think differently!!!
3. What stories / excuses or thoughts held you back in the last 12 months and didn't let you do what you wanted to do?

If the end of your life came, think that someone comes to show you how courageous you were all your life, full of vitality, and how you set an example to others by doing what you said you would without fearing anything! You did what you wanted! What you said you would do!

Now think about the opposite.
If the end of your life came and you were shown that you didn't do what you wanted and what you said you wanted to do because you were afraid... **what's worse?**
What would you do then?
How do you want to be remembered?
Like someone who did what he wanted to do and said he would or like someone who never did what he wanted to do?
 Forget the emotion (fear, insecurity, blah blah blah) that is holding you back and take action!!!
Look now are all those things that scared you still scare you the same after the 2 examples above (how you will be remembered)?
Luckily, you're still here so you don't have to say "I want to go back in time"! You are here! So, try, do them now!
Where are you with your business, health, money, relationship with others, the feeling of love, etc.?
Is it time to learn new skills?
Is it time for........(what?)
Do you allow yourself to feel happy now or do you say you will feel happy when you are successful?
Ask yourself these questions and answer them!

4. **Make a new story** (the one you tell every time you talk about your life, what you lived, and what you are living), and make new beliefs and new thoughts!
   Start something that gives you passion!
   Instead of thinking and reacting (your old story that you used to tell others) like "I'm too old now I can't..." , "I don't deserve...", "No one loved me....", "I didn't......"
  Change the way you think and react - change your story!!
   From "I'm Too old!"
   In "**I have more wisdom because I have so many years on me!**
   So, I have a lot to offer!"
   From "I'm fat and I'll be having such a hard time because of this for the rest of my life..." changed it to " **Because I have the experience of what it's like to be lets say fat... What obstacles a fat person has. How a fat person feels. What**

could help a fat person. **What stores have cheap clothes for fat people etc. I can help and I will make a page or videos with helpful instructions. Why not record my attempt to lose weight and improve my life and make it something like a diary and find others to start it together and motivate each other!"**
We change the things that were holding us back into positive statements!
Write what limits you and then write its positive.
Example:
I stress = **I thrive on pressure.**
I don't act because I'm waiting for the right moment to come = **when others are waiting for the right moment to come, I create, I do! OR I take action or take action when others are waiting!**
See what scares you as a strength, not an obstacle!
Say it again and again and in the end, you'll believe it!!
Tell your story the way you want, but positively with passion, and don't say what you didn't do and what scare you, those things belong in the past! Leave them behind you. **Stop talking about them. Stop using them**!

5. Where do you want to **be, have** now with your business, your health, your money, your relationship with others, the feeling of love, etc.? What are your goals on them?

****

6. **Think that a year has passed and it was the best time of your life. What should have happened for it to be the best time in your business, health, etc.?**
   Think that you are living it, that it happened! Think about them in detail and feel them!

****

Example of what we do wrong when we write our goal:

A) To simple say "I made so much money" or only say the amount is wrong. The right thing to say and think is something like that "I make so much (you write the amount). I am offering so much help... (how and where) and I feel so good. I feel proud to have passive income easily and (write how your life has changed for the better because of the money in details) ....". Don't just stay on the money. Describe how that has improved your life in details.
Another example:
B) I look at myself in the mirror: Look how beautiful I have become! I'm so proud of myself!

C) My book is ready and millions of people are holding it in their hands! Have read it and are talking to me about how much this or that chapter touched them and I feel so proud I am so moved by all this and…….
D) You won't say "I want to laugh more" but "I laugh so much I enjoy it!"
That kind of thinking and daydreaming is needed!
And that's how goals should be written!
Don't focus only on what you want but also on what you will offer to others. And on how your life will be affected by having your goal done!
Another example:
E) I help others overcome their traumatic experiences and finally become happy again. I feel so proud to see them remain happy, kind-hearted, and optimistic for the rest of their liveς!
F) I feel so proud of myself. I am so grateful, I have so much love in my life, I live and eat so healthily, I have 100,000 euros of income every month, some come from passive incomes and it keeps increasing in the most beautiful way.. I help my fellow human beings by using my earnings and I feel free! I am free from fears and anxieties and I enjoy my life completely and I laugh so much, I feel so much peace, joy, and gratitude. I have wonderful people around me ………..
****

And by answering all the above questions (in 1,2,3,4,5 and 6) and writing them you wrote your new goals! So easy and simple!
****

Read your goals every day so you don't fall into your bad routine again! And for not forgetting them!
****

When we write our goals and our wants, we have to find the deep reason that makes us want them.
To achieve this, we do the following:
 You have your first goal written down and you ask:
Why did I write this goal?
Why do I want to ….example get rich?
Whatever you answer you ask again: why do I want to… Let's say you wrote I want to be rich. Why? To have freedom. So, you ask why do I want to have freedom?
You continue to ask with the answer you gave - make your answer a question - I want to help = why do you want to help?
Because this makes me feel good = why does this make you feel good?
You must ask 7 different questions not less.
You do this for each one of your goals.

Each of our goals must be written completely and not half if we want to write them correctly.

Example: I want to have 50,000 euros every month as income because I want to have the freedom to live comfortably so that I can do…. enjoy… not just write a blank I want to have 50,000 euros every month as an income. There is a deeper reason why you want this and you need to write that down as well. I know for some it will be a very boring process but you do it once every 12 months it's not something you do every week!

And on the other hand, if you want to improve your life, stop making excuses and act! Here are the steps! Do them! Try them!

So why do you want to get where you want to go?
Why did you write this goal?
To get from where you are now to where you want to be, what do you need?
To shorten the distance and make it easier for you to reach your goal, what should you do?
Write down what you need to do every day.
What should you do in general too?
Example: Creating a new routine which will be what? A new way of thinking that will be how? Maybe practicing specific skills etc.
You must clarify within yourself why you want this goal! What makes you want it.

****

When we face something, yes, it is necessary for us to have a good strategy on how to solve it or at least on how to start. The right solution is needed but before that, we have to do something else first.
Let's think about what we think about ourselves. What is our current story that we tell ourselves and to others. Because what we believe about ourselves are also our beliefs! That is, if I say "nothing is going right in my life, I'm not worth it because I don't have money, how will they love me when I'm fat, etc." I focus on negative situations that have become my beliefs because that's how I see myself. **This is what-how I consider my life to be.**

I need to think about what is more important to me than feeling pain, humiliation, etc. So that this most important thing becomes my motivation to get out of this negative way of thinking that attracts what I am living now.

 First I have to see myself positively by changing my story beliefs so I can act on the solution with passion and without fear to succeed.

****

When we have low energy and we are constantly tired and constantly in a bad mood, we will not be able to go very far and succeed in life and we will not be able to successfully solve the difficulties that come our way.

To succeed in life, we must have vitality and energy. How will we achieve this?

See - act every day in everything you do, with intentionally feeling like when you fall in love. Yes, you read right! Intentionally show that kind of enthusiasm in everything you do! **See everything positively, and jump for joy**.
Consider the following:
When you're not in a good mood, how do you sit on the couch?
What is your posture?
If you talk to someone when you are not in a good mood, in what tone of voice and in what style will you say good morning and how are you? Will you answer: "Well... what can I say... let's say that I'm fine..."? Or "I am Crap dude what can I tell you now... who can be well in times like this»?

When you're in a good mood will you sink into your couch the same way you would if you were in a bad mood? Or will you sit straighter and more solidly?

When you are in a good mood when you meet someone or talk to someone, won't you respond more cheerfully and with positive words?

To manage to have so much energy and so much vitality even when you feel down is not as difficult as you think!

I won't break down the scientific part for you. Just try it!

Do the following as often as you can during the day:

Get up and jump around like crazy. Like you heard something wonderful.

Stretch yourself. Get up and stretch.

Speak with an enthusiastic tone.

Sit as you would if you were happy.

Make faces. Stretch your face by making funny faces.

Smile. Find ways to laugh many times throughout the day.

Don't sit around like you're sad.

Don't talk like you're sad.

Don't act like you're sad.

Try it.

Sit on the sofa more upright instead of sitting like a "sad Sunday".

As soon as you see that you start to get bored, and sleepy, and lose your concentration get up and dance again, and pretend you learned something spectacularly enjoyable!

Put on a song that really gets you in the mood and dance to it intensity and see how your mood will change for the better! There is a whole science behind it!

We have to change our posture and be like the heroes (superman, etc.) Notice how they stand. They do not stand miserable, and sad but with determination and vitality!

Do the following experiment to see if they are indeed right in what they say.

Try it when you're in a good mood to see the huge difference: while you're in a good mood sit like when you're angry, sad, or restless.

How long do you think you will remain cheerful if you adopt such a posture?

Try the opposite as well. While you are not in a good mood, take a dynamic posture and dance as if you won the lottery, smile, listen to your favorite song, and cheer. Are you still in the same bad mood?

Exercise somehow, go for a walk, or go for a run. It helps us. In the beginning, we start by forcing ourselves, but along the way, the fun builds up.
There is also a special type of very simple exercise that helps to gain energy and activate the body, but also to get rid of general physical pains. This method is the **egoscue method** - Brian Bradley Tony Robbins. Look it up! Type it into google exactly like that and it will bring up a video for you to watch.
****

In order to succeed in your life, you must act with enthusiasm even when you feel afraid!
And you have to identify your negative beliefs and change them!
Otherwise, you will take one step forward and two steps back. You will wonder for a lifetime why things never go well for you. **Stop living just to survive and start living to succeed*!*￼**
****

Most of us do a lot more when it comes to helping someone than when it comes to helping ourselves! We are activated when it comes to helping another! Use that!

****

We must invest in constantly improving ourselves, with seminars, by learning new skills, by reading books.

Because this investment is not taxable, but also because what we learn gives us knowledge that will help us to solve our problems more wisely and we will be able to exist professionally over time.

To be able to have such a mentality you must have energy and vitality!

Dwelling on your negative emotions only keeps you away from success, from acting and away from a better quality of life!

****

Think if at some point in your life, something inside you changed and you succeeded and did the turnaround (you must at least have one such moment)!
You stopped fearing or putting up with something and said: "This is enough!" and you changed something in your life.
What was the situation you were dealing with for a long time until at some point you couldn't take it anymore and made the change?

What was it that prompted you to make the necessary changes that you didn't dare to make for so long?

What was the moment that changed everything?

What was that something that pushed you to say no more and act accordingly?

What made you keep this change and not go back to the old ways again?

New beliefs?
Perhaps an inner awakening?
What?

Learn yourself. Think of all the times you managed to change something and **write it down**! It will help you get courage and strength and see how you did it then, so you know how to do it now!

 It's not impossible after all you've done it before! Learn from how you did it back then.

****

In the past I used to think I was ………… (Ugly, failed, not enough, etc.) but now I choose to believe…………that (I am worthy, I am enough, I am lovable, life is good, etc.)

This new statement-belief must be said or read **15 times during the day** so that the brain and the subconscious begin to connect it with what you want and delete the negative thought-belief.

The fact that now you choose how you think and how you act and you are no longer on autopilot, stuck in the past, your subconscious is being led in new directions that are current and optimistic.

****

How we see ourselves must match who we want to be. Our beliefs, what we say about ourselves and our lives our hobbies, and our habits, must match who we want to be.

We must leave our old selves behind and see our improved selves. We must focus on everything we do.

If we keep saying negative things about ourselves, about our lives, and about life in general, nothing is going to change. You are unfairly waiting for something to change.

We must change our bad habits. Put new ones that push us to our best selves! **New hobbies, new coping and reaction strategies for the difficult, and for how we see life itself and ourselves!**

****

There are three keys that lead us to make the desired change:

1. How we feel.
2. What story do we believe and tell about ourselves and our lives.
3. Our Strategy: The plan of action designed to achieve our major or overarching goal.

Our story is the glue that holds us tightly together either with our limiting beliefs that hold us back or with what motivates us to action.

How you feel controls what you focus on.
What you focus on creates your story.
Your story directs your strategy (how well you can find solutions and how to move forward with your life).

We do not experience life itself with its joys and its gifts. **We experience the life we think it is as it is because we only focus on individual events that hurt us and that we experienced them much more intensely than they were.**

****

Only one moment in time is enough to change everything. When the impossible becomes possible.

To do something and change your life all you need is 5 seconds of courage. That's all it takes for us to say "That's enough" and the click is made inside us that pushes us to change!

If in some area of your life, you insist on focusing on the pain you feel about that part of your life, think of this: **Is there anything else that is more important to you than suffering? Is there anything more important than insisting on remembering and thinking about what it was that once caused you this pain?**

Example: Is being able to help others worth more? Being able to travel? Your child? Raising your child, etc.? Isn't this more important to make you say "I wasted so many years of my life being stuck in (your suffering) …... when I could be traveling, which I love so much and want to experience. Or I am stuck and wasting time from spending time with my child who needs me…..etc.?" Is it worth losing the opportunity to do what you want because you think about all the old stuff that once hurt you?

****

Write them down! Don't get bored!
Find out how you are sabotaging yourself and what your negative beliefs are and let's change them!

1. What would be the first step you could take now to commit to these new goals of yours?

2. What's your old story?

3. And what labels-negative beliefs do you tell to yourself?

Example: "If I don't achieve this, I'm not enough" …... **If I don't……. then I am not** ……..

4. **How you feel is what drives you to what story you will tell and what you believe about yourself and your life!**

5. When you are angry you remember everything the other person did that made you angry. Unlike when you are in love you see the good in the other person and you

don't pay so much attention to what bothers you. _Do you understand the difference?_ That's why it's so important to improve how you react! That's why it's so important to act like you're in love and happy!

6. **You look for what you already believe in**.

7. Most changes for the better start with changing your story. **Change your story (in your mind and when you tell it to others) so that the worst day becomes the best day of your life. Change your story, change your life**.

8. Having the wrong story in our mind because we overlived it and we no longer have the real facts in our mind but our overreaction of the pain or fear, we fail to see the solution and the positive of the whole situation.

9. Divorce your story of limitation (focusing on what you think you can't do and what you've failed at) and marry the truth of your unlimited ability (focus on what you know, what you can learn, what you can offer!).

10. **Stop telling yourself and everyone the wrong story over and over again**!!

11. Your limiting beliefs are holding you back. "Tried everything"...really?! If you had tried everything you would have achieved what you wanted. Find them and change them (your negative beliefs) so you don't take one step forward and two steps back!

12. How to do it is usually not the problem but that we don't act and spend our time only researching and worrying.

Example: You want to lose weight because you are overweight. You start looking for what diet is out there. Then you look to find the best fitness program. You don't start walking a little bit and then a little bit more while you search for the perfect program and for the perfect diet. But you continue to eat as before and sit for hours.
Start with simple walking, don't take the elevator, and cut out the sodas and the heavy dinner while you do your research!

You don't need the perfect program as long as you take action and change your routine! **Too many people get overwhelmed with so much information and never get started**!

13. It's not enough to know what to do... you have to execute it. You won't get results without action.

14. For example becoming wealthy will not bring you happiness by itself. Who you become as a person (how much you change for the better or for the worse) because you've succeeded will make you happy or not.

Example: If you don't have friends even though you became rich. If you don't know how to manage so much money so you don't go broke. If you don't discover what you really need... you won't be happy even if you achieve your goal of becoming rich.

15. Be a guard of your mind! Don't allow negative emotions to nest! **Stop them as they first appear!**

16. Your biggest problem is that you think you shouldn't have problems. You don't see every problem as an opportunity for development but you get scared and get trapped in it.

17. Everyone experiences some kind of stress. The point is how to manage it creatively.

18. You can be satisfied and happy only through your personal growth.

****

Now let's go to a technique:

If you feel like you are stuck in your life. If you feel so angry all the time or disappointed etc. And you can't move forward do the following: (let's, say you have no idea what to write in your new book, or you don't know what you want from your life, etc.)

Stand up and do the following exercise:

Every time you will change "assistant" shake your body intensely to disconnect from one "assistant" so you can connect to another "assistant".

Say that a fighter lives inside you.

 In which part of your body does it live?

The first place that you will think or feel that the fighter inside you lives there, put your hand there. Don't take your hand keep it there. Then make the sound a fighter makes, make it intense, live it!

Then think about your problem and ask:

Fighter Calliope (say your name) what should I do? What should I focus on and what should I remember about this situation? (You ask this three times). Something will spring out of you, that's for sure. An idea, a memory, something.

Then think that a witch (magician if you are a man) lives inside you.

At the first point where you will think or feel that the witch (magician) lives inside you, put your hand there. Keep your hand there. Then make the sound a witch makes, do it strongly, live it! Whatever sound you feel your wizard or witch makes.

Then think about your problem and ask:

Witch (wizard) Calliope (say your name) what should I do? What should I focus on and what should I remember about this situation? (You ask this 3 times).

Then you think that a lover lives inside you.

Feel in which part of the body it lives and put your hand there and make the sound of a man or a woman in love!

Then do the steps you did above.

Then think that inside you live **a queen (a king if you are a man)** and do the above.

Then you get each "helper" to ask the next "helper" what they have to say about your problem as if they were talking to each other about your problem.

Example: Fighter Calliope what does the Witch have to say on this topic? Fighter Calliope what does the lover have to say on this matter? Fighter Calliope what does the queen have to say on this matter? Witch Calliope what does the fighter have to say on this matter? Witch Calliope what does love have to say on this matter? Witch Calliope what does the queen have to say on this matter? Lover, what does the fighter have to say on this matter? Etc.

This technique helps you to listen to what yourself, your soul, and your being want to tell you about **how to overcome something and what is preventing you from overcoming it for so long.** It can be a time-consuming process but it is worth it.

Let's say a little more about these "helpers".

The Fighter: Nothing will stop him or her. He doesn't give up on anything. He is the protector within us.

The Magician: Never stress, never worry about anything because this part of you knows that everything is just a story that can change at any time. This part of you has a lot of humor and likes to be playful.

Lover: He or she loves life and everything he does he does it with love. He attracts people and situations and things into his life. This part of you is compassionate and connected to everything.

The queen, king: It is the heart of the service. This part of us has all the wisdom and helps us grow (improve) and deliver. It is a won place. The way this part of you thinks is: I may lose the battle, but I will win the war... I'm not trying to get; I'm trying to take care of others.

No matter how boring or ridiculous it seems to you when you find yourself in a difficult situation (even when you can't get rid of a strong negative feeling and you've been carrying it for months or you've run out of ideas... or when some physical pain won't go away after you've tried everything) try it and I promise I won't tell it anywhere, it will be our secret! No one will know to make fun of you!

 This technique was told by Tony Robbins in his free seminar *Become Unshakeable 2023 Challenge.*

****

So, what do you need to be happy?

To be motivated to move forward you need to have a bright future.

If you think of your future as miserable and full of pain, you won't have the desire to wake up and improve. You will not want to learn from seminars and books how to achieve in your life the best that you deserve.

if you have a great goal that you positively focus on then you will have the appetite to improve and learn and act!

Your goals must be detailed and clear and you must focus on them positively.

 And don't forget we should always give much more than we expect to get.

****

We return to the most basic part on how we can achieve our goals.

 The strongest force in human personality is the need to remain consistent with how we define ourselves (what we believe about ourselves, the good and the bad).

If I say that I am a failure at the end of the day I will feel like a failure and the circumstances that I will experience will be such that they will confirm this false belief that I have about myself.
That's why it's so important to find out what our identity is - our story - our beliefs.
If we tell a lie many times and passionately others will believe it. That's how it is with us. We put different labels on ourselves because we once happened to act in a way that we didn't like, offended us, or because that's how someone characterized us for a long time and now, we say it non-stop that this is who we are and we believe it. By

acting like that we are putting a limitation on what we can do. If we don't get rid of these labels, we will stay with them.

If, for example, we get excited about an idea that came to us and at the last moment we are filled with fear and hesitate and we do this again and again we will label ourselves "I am a procrastinator"...»

Let's think, what role do we play in our personal story?
The victim;
He who only satisfies others;
The oppressor or exploiter:
Someone who imposes his will on others?
The critic?
The spacer or isolator?
The guide or mentor?
The Savior?
The analyst or the philosopher?
The creator or artist?
The volunteer?
The one who says yes to everything? Etc.

When we tell what we experienced to others and to ourselves, what role do we have in this story?
You have to find out what your old identity is and create a new one.

What things control us? - what controls our emotional house?

If we are not having a good time, if we are not feeling well, even one minute seems endless.
We return to our home even if it is not nice, we return to our thoughts even if they are full of pain and negativity. We exist in our bodies even if we don't like them. We can't help but come home to both our thoughts and our bodies.
Even if we don't like ourselves and our life, is our home and we can't help but go back to it.
But we can improve them in order to like them! It's never too late!

Many things will make you better in the short term. Just don't go back to the old ways. When you blame and you diminish yourself you diminish your energy. Without energy and a good mood, you cannot change. You are trapped in a vicious circle. The more you blame and put yourself down the worse it makes you feel... causing you to blame and put yourself down even more.

****

If you count the days since you started a change … you still haven't changed.
How can you tell if someone will stick with and overcome an "addiction" (such as smoking, dieting, etc.) or if they will succeed in changing a wrong mindset?
You ask him "how is he doing" or if they ask him for example "do you smoke?"
If he answers: "I'm on the 7th day of not smoking or I have 3 months and 3 days of..." and he doesn't say "I don't do that or I don't belong to that category of people or I don't smoke" then he will roll again because he counts the days and this shows that the will to achieve it has not taken roots in him.
 He hasn't changed his belief. Maybe this time he will hold his effort a little longer than the previous effort he had made.

****

Your identity decides what you are looking for!

Depending on what you believe about yourself, you also decide what you deserve and what you don't deserve.
You decide what you need and what you don't need.
Identity is the way that leverages everything and is the fastest way to lasting change.
Identity: **who do you think you are and who do you think you are not?** Sit down and write it.
Our decisions are controlled by our identity.
Your identity determines how you interact with other people and how they interact with you.

Example:
"He is a generous man" - warm, kind, a friend... How much does this determine how you interact with this person when you think of him or her like that?
"She's a manipulative bitch" - how much does that determine how you interact with that person when you see her like that?
Identity: a set of beliefs associated with a person.

On the other hand, if a friend treats us badly, we will think "come on he just had a bad day" since he generally treats us well.
While someone who generally treats us badly, if he treats us well, we won't think "oh, he's in a good mood today, although that rarely happens." But we will say "oh he must want something from me now".

So, the way you interact with someone is not only controlled by the person but by the identity we have given to that person.

If you have put in the identity of who you are an example: "I always lose." This belief of yours is so strong that you can attend 5000 seminars and still have your life remain the same because you will self-sabotage your efforts.
Because the brain just goes on and lives with what you taught it. And in this example that is "no matter what you do, you will always come out a loser in the end"

A trick: When you say something out loud, with full force, intensity, enthusiasm, and movement: you imprint it on your identity... it's like hypnotizing yourself. Try it to instill positive beliefs deep within yourself.

Example: Find a calm and quiet place and stand in front of a mirror. Then repeat out loud and with full force the phrase "**I am capable and have the power to achieve anything I want.**" Repeat the phrase several times with passion and movement so that it is imprinted in your mind and identity. **Make movements with your body. Movements of determination, strength, vitality, etc.**

 We need to change our identity!
Let's not forget that people are not their behaviors.
We can all reach states of rage, anger, and depression as a result of which we behave badly, and abruptly for a long time.

****

Why we fail:

Let's take the example of money. We are used on having a specific among of money. If you get to have more all of a sudden then you start sabotaging yourself until you go back to how you are used to.

Until we change our identity, we have no permanent change. If you don't get what you want, it's just a reflection of who you are.

Is it time to redefine who I am?

Your identity affects your entire life. Change your life...change your story. It starts with who you think you are because if you don't know who you are...you don't know what to do. You create a new identity with actions.

We don't do what we can, we do what we think we are.

Example:

If we say that we are not capable or that we are not very intelligent, when we go to do something, we will not give our best, we will not do it with love. And we will either do it wrong or give up because we will find it difficult when it may not be that difficult.

 If we say we want to become rich but we envy those who win the jackpot or those who have money and we say that money makes people arrogant and bad or if we are wasteful or if we have not made a clear plan what we would do with the money if we became rich, then in the first cases money will never come to us and in the last cases we will waste it and become poor again if we got rich.

The fastest way to change how I feel is to radically change my body.

How do I make a radical change to stop feeling and thinking something negative: run, dance, move, shout, sing, take a cold shower……..the brain will start working differently. You will be forced to focus on different thinking.

If you focus on what you don't have…..if you keep focusing on it…how can you achieve happiness? How can you cheer yourself up if you focus on what you don't have?

Successful people don't think or talk about what they don't have.

Also, those who succeed enjoy the now, and the today and foresee the future to make it better.

If we get stuck thinking about what we lack for each of our goals and we fail to achieve them, this is not a lack of resources but a lack of resourcefulness.

Instead of thinking of creative ways to bypass or gain or create new paths to what is missing, you become discouraged and give up. You are thinking that there are so many obstacles or that you are not capable of achieving them.

****

The words we attribute to our experience become our experience. The words we use change our biochemistry. Words can escalate our emotions.

Example: "nutritious snack" / "delicious snack", "very nice person" / "playful person" / "sexy person" ... different meanings = we get different feelings depending on the sentence.

You will feel different if someone tells you this is a nutritious snack and different when they tell you this is a tasty snack. You will feel and react differently to someone you consider a very good person and to someone you consider a very sexy person.

****

You need compelling goals.

If your goals are uninspired, you don't feel inspired.

If you don't have something to excite you, you will give up and be miserable.

Anyone can face their horrible today if they know that an exciting tomorrow awaits them and focus on their goal.

****

If you have the mindset "There is a way!" then you will always find it!

****

Why it is important to offer to others:

When we grow up, we have things to give to people we love or even to strangers. That can change our lives. It gives meaning to our lives! You get out of your microcosm and out of your problems. You get so much joy from helping that it fills your being! You are filled with the love and joy from those that you are helping! You stop feeling alone!

****

If you haven't done it, do it now! Write:
What was my old identity?
What is my new identity?
Who are you really at your core?
What will this new identity create for you? (Example: Much more confidence in myself).

****

Show who you are - not only in words, but also in actions.

Find something you can do for your community / city / neighborhood. Something that is necessary. Something that will give joy. Something that will solve a problem.

Change identity by doing things - actions outside of what you would normally do. Get out of your comfort zone!

And as a professional, this will help you. You will promote your work. You won't advertise that you did it, let them find out for themselves so you don't look like you only care about showing off. Do good without saying it. They will find out that you did it and they will see you in a very positive way because you didn't brag about it.

Examples: Plant flowers on the sidewalks. Put ecological lighting on a dark street. Put houses and food for the stray kitties. Build a small playground for the children to play and enjoy. Beautify your area in some way. **See the needs that exist and act accordingly.**

If you don't try what you read you won't get anything out of this book and everything will just be the same as before you read it.

****

When we don't succeed even though we say we think positively we need to pay attention to our contradictory beliefs and our contradictory words that cause us to take one step forward and 2 steps back.

Example 1: I want to be happy without anyone being sad. But this is not always possible and someone will be jealous of your success.

Example 2: You love your wife and you tell everyone about it. But you also say the following "<u>I am chained to a marriage</u>", and "<u>life is a battle</u>". And because you will say something so negative, (Because you say that life is a battle!) you will experience a difficult everyday life. And since you say that you are chained to a marriage, you end up not showing your love to your wife as much as you think you do and you get very angry with her all the time. You constantly focusing seeing her negatives. In the end all you will see is: your wife and life itself as an unbearable burden.

Example 3: Why don't you find the right partner? Because you say and probably believe it "<u>there are no good men out there</u>". You will attract men who will not respect you since you say there are no men out there. Maybe you started saying it after some bad relationships, but you made it a belief and didn't think positively back then. **You didn't think that after every failed relationship:** You learned how to appreciate good behavior. You also learned yourself. And now you are ready to appreciate the other person without unreasonable demands.

Thought: I want to have a fun and enjoyable life. Contradictory thought: But I don't want to suffer the consequences of my actions and experience the consequences afterwards.

Do you see the big difference in the way of thinking?

This also happens in our various expressions such as "life is a battle, I'm always alone, I've never been loved, I have no money (you'll never have money left, something will happen and you'll have to spend it all since you say I don't have!)" etc.

Change those labels you put on yourself and others. Accept that it was just lessons, nothing more. They do not characterize you and they do not characterize life either (how life is and how life treats you and how life brings you everything).

****

Telling our children «You're beautiful, you're perfect, etc." it doesn't help them much because if they go out in life and someone tells them «How ugly you are or something ugly" they will be shocked and their self-esteem will be hurt too much because they don't know how to handle such situations. They didn't learn how not to take other people's bad comments personally. They lived in an environment where everyone was treating them too nicely.

We must reward the effort children make in everything.

Well done for trying and not giving up!
Well done for trying and succeeding... even if you only got to the beginning.
Well done!
Good job!
You are very smart!
You are very skilled!
Keep going!
I like that you're trying!
Nice try!
I was impressed by how hard you worked!
You are to be congratulated for your effort!
You are really dedicated to what you do!
I love that you don't give up easily and keep trying!
I see you've improved a lot since the last time you tried!
It's obvious how much passion you have for what you do!
You are very careful and/or precise in the performance of your tasks!
Looks like you're really trying hard!
Keep trying like this and you will achieve your goal!
I'm proud of how hard you try!
It's nice to see someone working hard like you!
You are very skilled at what you do!
You have made great progress!
I love seeing how hard you try to improve!

****

If you say "I can't do that" (and I am not saying go jump off a cliff) that's when you need to do it in order to empower yourself. If you give in to your fears, you will end up becoming fearless, miserable, etc. You will put a lot of limiting labels/beliefs on you. Dare while afraid. For example, say you are afraid to go up and speak to a lot of people, and instead of giving up you do it, you will feel stronger! You will be filled with confidence! And if you do this again and again, imagine how much stronger as a person you will feel and become!

****

Say loudly and strongly what you want from your life. Bring your words to life! Go for a run and like crazy (well, do it at home or on a mountain or deep in the sea) say for example **I'm worth it!!! I am too**………. and fill in what you want!

****

Technique: How to instantly change how negatively you started to feel about something.

A) Don't let your negative feeling grow, catch them in the beginning. Our body can help us with this! Get up and wave your arms like crazy. Get up and dance hard. Get up and make crazy expressions. Shake your body and face vigorously! This will fill you with energy as well as cheer you up.

B) Close your eyes and think of something positive (with or without music) for example something you are grateful for and shake your body vigorously with your eyes closed. Then express equally loudly with faces and sounds. Live it!

Don't you feel better now?

****

When we say positive statements, we should not say for example I want to have or acquire 40 million. **We have to state why we want them**. In this way you give and feel an emotion to your goal and you give more positive energy to it.

Example: I want to have 40 million because I want my freedom to ……….
I want this because……………………………

Example: My goal is to spend the day…. Or Get through each day easily……. *This is incorrect*. If you say my goal is to fill people with my presence and spread joy and…. *the difference is huge*! You will be filled with events that will improve you as a person so that you can complete this goal of yours! A simple "I want to get on with my day" is a miserable and negative expression of a person who has given up on himself. What must happen so you can consider that your day was easy, pleasant, worthwhile? Why do you want your day to be easy? **Describe how you want it to be in details!**

If, for example, you complain that your every day is so hard, you expressing yourself in a fatalistic way like "let's get through this day too", "my goal is to get through the day", "let this day go too" etc. You are definitely going to have a hard day if you express yourself in such a negative way!

****

Start now! Focus on a positive goal. Think and say that what you are experiencing now is nothing in front of what you will experience soon, when you will be reaching your goal! So you don't pay too much attention and get stuck exaggerating how bad your now is.

****

Also, **don't say negative words** like: I'm depressed, I feel sad, I was betrayed, etc. **By putting labels on yourself and on various situations you magnify them and cling to them.**
It's not the end of the world with what you went through, everything can be fixed and everything has something positive to teach us.
 If we focus on and exaggerate the problem, how will you overcome it?

****

As a professional or worker, don't focus on your lack of education and skills as an excuse not to dare and believe in yourself and what you know. **Offer what you know how to do well**!

****

You want to get more customers, build a name, and be trusted.

More important is to build trust first. Offer something for free without spreading the word that you did it and wait and see! They will find out and start to trust your name.

For example, in your neighborhood (yes, start from there!) the place is full of garbage due to a strike or there is no greenery or something is missing.... if you have the money or know how to do it yourself, go do it or pay someone to do it! Let people find out that you did it and you will see that people will speak positively about you and feel confident about you.

If you don't have anything to offer related to your work, offer something unrelated but very useful and necessary!

Also, consider the following:
What do you provide that others know that when they need it, they will definitely find it to you?
If someone asks you why I should prefer you and not someone else, what will you answer?
What unique thing do you have to offer that others don't?

Let's talk a little about how you can grow your business no matter what you do:
1. Get to know very well who your customers are, and your audience.
   What kind of customers do you want (think of them in details)? (That can be a goal)
2. Offer something unique and exceptional. (If you do not have make a goal to find it)

What do you have to offer that no one else does?
3. Offer and deliver much more than the customer expects to receive.
   What extra (free) can you add to each purchase each customer will make?
   What unique offer can you offer your customers?
   Sit down and write your answers! Take your time, think, and answer!

Observe others who succeed.
What do they do so differently from the rest that makes them successful?
What do they do - offer differently and their turnover - clientele - appreciation for them is increasing?

What do they offer and how?

Build it, sell it, increase the product's readability or your own. Focus only on what brings return on investment. Start small, think big and scale quickly. People want to start with big steps and end up never starting.

Fall "in love" with your customers - with your products and services and change and improve them if it is needed.

When the customer trusts you then you can evolve. The customer trusts you because he sees that the services and the product are offered with love and respect and that something extra is always given. That's why he will stay with you. Business is a mental game. You need to know how people think and react.

Give something first and add value. Become more valuable to people who need something specific that you can provide! If you add more value than anyone else, you will dominate the market. Learn what people need and how you can become incredibly valuable.

Think:

Who can I do more for?
For their pain?
What kind of pain can I provide relief for?
For their needs?
For what kind of need can I offer a convenience?
For their desires?
For what kind of desire can I offer a product, or a service?
For their doubts?
For what kinds of doubts of my fellow men can I offer solutions?
Find a way to add value!!! "Offer identity to people through what's on offer."
Be persistent in seeking better ways to meet the needs of your fellow human beings / customers.

Business is something spiritual!! For the people you fell in love with and for yourself, you always do the best and want the best! Think of your customers as the ones you love and as being you. So, what will you offer to yourself or to your loved ones?
So, give - offer more with quality and this way you will create enthusiastic fans => brand => your business will have an identity and as a result customers will look for you.
Never stop looking for better ways to give your customers what they need!
Make people want to work with you - buy from you. Do something that has so much value to people and advertise it, and then customers will tell it to everyone they know.
It's easier to do marketing today because of the internet. Find the right people - customers - your audience to serve!

****

Three things you should do in any job and whatever you are doing and you can also apply them to your relationships.

1. Discover who your ideal customer is.

Who your lover is as a character. Take the time to learn them!

The customers who will buy something simply because the store happened to be on their street they will buy and leave. The customers who stay and will buy again and again are those who are looking to find something specific (service or product) from a professional or from a specialized organization (a specific brand).

Who is the person – the customer who will buy during a pandemic in the midst of difficult times from you? (What do they like? What do they dislike? What are their habits?......)

Who buys repeatedly?

Who will tell others about your product/service?

Find these people - customers and find out what they want and how they want it.

Who can I do the most for?
For what class of people?
For what phobia or difficulty can I offer something as relief or ease?
"Life is the dance between what you desire most and what you fear." **Increase desire or decrease fear, yours and your customers.**

2. What is your irresistible offer?

What can you offer to your lover that can lift them? Help them be the best version of themselves!

An offer that's so good, the person/customer will feel lame if they don't take it!

3. **Deliver more - Give more!**

Give more than they expect to receive. Make it personal. Example: Don't deliver shoes... deliver happiness. Put something extra in the box that will make the customer smile. Make the box, the receipt, the whole experience very pleasant and why not add humor.

The right professional thinks:

Let me understand you and appreciate you and feel you. Let me see if there is a way to ease your pain or improve your life. Let me make you an offer so irresistible you won't be able to resist. And let me go overboard and give you a gift as well.

****

When we make positive statements, the difference is huge when you say: I feel excited! From saying I'm excited! You have to do the corresponding physical movements that you would do when you are really excited and happy.

Let your body participate and add the corresponding tone of voice.

Only the combination of **positive words + movement of enthusiasm + voice of enthusiasm + constant repetition = positive statements will begin to take root in us and become believed.**

 That's why with our goals we must talk about them to ourselves a lot and to the right people. And we must think of them with enthusiasm and determination and continuity.

****

What do you say to yourself when you feel angry with yourself for something you did?

What you say is what you think about yourself! It's the labels you've put on yourself!

Example: I'm dumb, I'm too old, I'm.......

Sit down and write them! Learn them so you can fix them!

****

Focus better on what you say about yourself when you are at your best! When you feel proud of yourself! When you are happy! When you've accomplished something! **Sit down and write what you say to yourself at your best! And use them as positive statements. Read them every day.**

Example: "My Goddess! You did it again!" etc.

****

Write what is your story that you have been telling all these years **now**. And what is your new story without judging yourself, without characterizing yourself negatively. The labels that you put are unfair because you are still learning and you will make mistakes. When you put them on it was too early and you had no experience. All of the *I'm lazy, I'm sensitive, I'm ....* how sure are you that you are all of these things? Without labels, you can be even more because labels limit you and stop you from being all that you can be.

****

Start being grateful for what you have. Stop associating things and situations with negative feelings and negative thoughts and start associating them with gratitude.

****

To succeed in life you need vitality, energy, and enthusiasm. You cannot have these with negative thoughts and negative feelings.

Think about not having a home, not hearing, not being able to see, not being able to remember, being disabled, living in a war country and not having electricity and heat and food .... there is always worse than what you are experiencing. Every day when you wake up and at night when you lie down, think with gratitude about what you have! Be thankful write/think about all the beautiful, positive things that happened in the day and what you have in general.

****

Fear and all negative emotions keep us away from our best selves, away from solutions, away from our abilities, away from being inspired.

****

Act! Don't make things too complicated so you will be confused and not act. Simplify it!

****

What am I willing to do to make my dreams come true? What;
****

We all have the ability to create a rich life on our own terms and provide more value.
****

80% of wealth is psychology (attitude, how you use things in your mind, what belief system you have, your movements/actions...) and only 20% is how you use money.
****

People have an internal rejection and pain for wealth and judge badly those who have money. Examples: "money is bad", "he's rich, who knows what scams he used to get so much money", "yes, he found them ready from his father", "if you don't work like a dog", etc. Work on yourself and delete those limited ways of thinking and talking!

****

To make more money you have to find ways to add more value for others (give others something very good that they need). **Notice the difficulties and eases of each year. What opportunities have they created? How can you create something that will serve even a certain portion of people?**

****

Money is not evil, money is there to be used to contribute to our fellow man.

****

If you add more **value** you will grow! What you offer, whether it is a service or a product, if it is **top quality**, with **love** and **respect** for the customer, **you cannot fail**.

****

Source of continuous income to exist you must connect your intelligence with the purpose of your life.

****

There is one path to success and this is: The more people you try to support, the more life and insight -experience you gain.

****

The "What will I gain if I help / if I do this" mentality is so wrong that it leads to failure.

****

If you don't know what fills you and what could fill you with passion, ask yourself the following:

1. What makes you cry?
2. What makes you feel calm?
3. What makes you forget yourself and not care about anything?
4. What means more to you than any business - any job?
5. What makes you sad?

Sit down and write your answers!

****

How you manage your stress also determines the quality of life you will have. **What do you do, what do you think, and how do you react** when life is unfair?
Start thinking: "I am the creator of my life, not the manager of my circumstances."

****

Techniques to calm your panic and any negative emotion you have.

The first two were shown to me by an amazing person who helps me by doing emotional energy healing to me to get rid of my negatively trapped emotions from all those years.

A huge thanks to https://despina-charavgi.carrd.co/?fbclid=IwAR2mdhw7ldA7mIYATOjEhfbwaUDGHg5BPKhinrKGohLl HVHyMYHdoQC9DIw **for showing them and now I have a very good weapon against my strong negative emotions!**

1. https://youtu.be/nl2dZMJmM1w:
   With this method you will calm your anger and all your negative emotions. This method of course does a lot more and its normal form requires you to invest around 15 to 20 minutes of your time and close your eyes and imagine a certain scenario (paul mckenna- the having technique – find his video on YouTube to see if you want the whole process). But even in the fast format, the results you can get will be just as important. Just touch yourself like in the video I made for you and then with your head still move your eyes left and right. When I did the whole process afterwards, I was filled with so much energy!! I was very impressed.
2. https://youtu.be/X_wCVcmS_pc :
   This method is much simpler and faster. You simply touch your body from your neck to your navel as many times as necessary until the panic, the negative feeling you are experiencing is reduced. When I do it I feel calm I feel loved.
3. https://youtu.be/It4aZkiAudM :
   There is a technique called ho oponopono (I am sorry, I love you, please forgive me, thank you).
   I won't tell you who came up with it and stuff like that. You can look this up yourself.
   I will tell you how you can use it to give a positive energy and find a solution to any problem you have.
   You can apply it at any time of the day and for as long as you want.
   If you start making excuses that you don't have time then try it when you go to sleep.
   Think about the problem that concerns you (the bad relationship with your child, with your boss or neighbor. Some health problems of yours or someone you love. Some work or money problem. Etc.) and evaluate how it has affected you.
   Then just say "I'm sorry, I love you, please forgive me, thank you at least 3 times.

If you want to go deeper you can the first time, say the words and think about the problem example: **I'm sorry, forgive me for everything that happens inside me and causes my life to** be sick, unhappy, fat, in pain, without income, etc.

The second time you can say for example if it has to do with someone you have a bad relationship with "I don't want us to hurt each other like that….. and you say the words/phrases we said.

And on the third time think of something again related to the problem and what you regret and then put sorry, I love you, please forgive me, thank you. The more time you spend on it, the faster the results will come.

4. https://youtu.be/ppkozWhzk0s: Emotional Freedom Technique.
   In this way you banish any negative emotion - belief! I tried it and I was so surprised!

If suddenly something makes you feel angry or anxious or jealous or I don't know what try it. If you believe that you are not worthy, that because you do not have money you are not worthy, **that you are not**……. Whatever negative belief you have just try it!

I will give you a picture that shows the places where you will "hit" with your fingers: on your face, your palm, and on your chest.

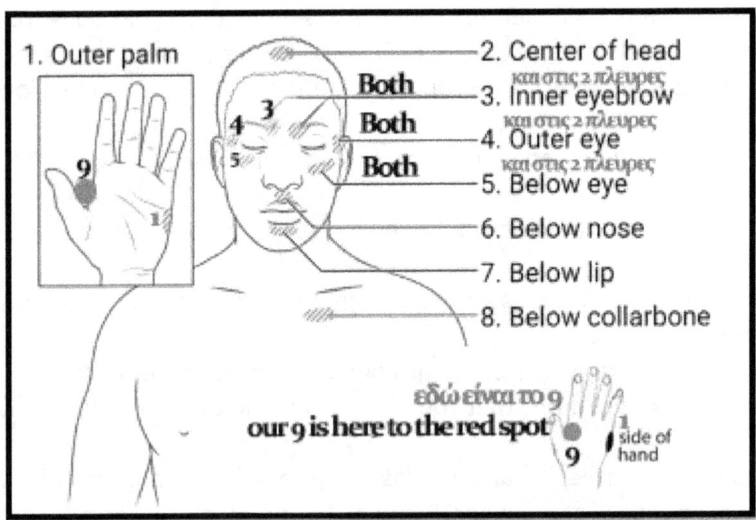

We start by thinking about what belief / negative emotion we want to banish.

 As an example, I'll use the phrase "I'm not good enough."

We take the fingers of one hand and knock hard (not to hurt but like knocking on the front door for someone who doesn't have a bell) on point 1 and say **"even if I don't feel good enough or even though I feel like I'm not good enough, I love me deeply, I accept me as I am or I accept myself as I am..** Say it 3 times. You keep hitting point 1 as you say this 3 times. <u>Tap each point 7 times with a slow steady rhythm and with your fingers.</u>
Example:
Even though I feel like I'm not enough, I love and accept myself
Or
I love and accept myself, even though I feel like I'm not enough.
Or
Even though I feel like I'm not good enough, I love and accept myself just the way I am. Say it 3 times and tap 7 times fast.

Then you go to point number 2 at the top of the head and hit saying only the core of this belief is "good enough". You say it at least 3 times and hit 7 times. "Good enough, good enough good enough»

Then you go to point 3 between your 2 eyes and tap 7 times on both sides simultaneously and say at least 3 times your core phrase which in our example is "Good enough, good enough good enough».

You can say your core phrase as many times as you like as you hit the points it does good and not bad. Just don't overdo it and get bored and feel that this technique is taking up too much of your time.

Then go to point 4 on the side of your eyes and make it contemporary on both sides saying as described above.

Then go to point 5 which is below your eyes and tap on both sides simultaneously saying your phrase 3 times. As we described at the beginning.

Then go to point 6 which is right under your nose and do the same as you did to the other points.

Then go to point 7 which is under your lips and do as we have said.

Then at point 8 and do what we said.

Point 9 is on your palm on the outside and near the big finger.

Point 9 in this variation of the technique is as I show you in the photo but the normal technique places it elsewhere. We are not concerned with that here because I am showing you this variation.

It's a good idea to do all these steps 3-4 times to make sure you got what you wanted. When I try it the 3rd time, I felt lighter and like a weight was lifted off me and when I said the whole sentence, I felt like I don't need it because I don't believe that anymore! Don't forget tap 7 times in each point fast!

The 3 and 4 I first read it from Joe Vitale. Look him up on Google and YouTube he has a lot of interesting things to tell you! Also, Brad Yates has great videos on the Emotional Freedom Technique they are worth it!

****

Every time you expand your abilities your worst days can become the best days of your life. Because you feel more proud of yourself. Because you are filled with vitality. You are putting yourself out of your misery.

****

When there is any crisis, we are forced to think differently and we try new things that's why many opportunities arise.

****

 When you think that everything you do, you do it for yourself, you will also be gripped by fear and various other things. When you say I do it for others, you are filled with courage and boldness.

****

Find why you want to do what you want, to find the unshakable motivation within you that will lead you until the end with courage and boldness.

****

Relationships with colleagues, children, friends, partners, etc.:

Now you will probably tell me what this has to do with goals. A lot. Because even being rich you always seek to connect with others and having good relationships with those around you and having a great partner bring you unlimited joy.

What else can get you so high as falling in love?

Every relationship is an opportunity to learn.

The quality of your life is the quality of your relationship with yourself, the universe, family, friends, colleagues, clients, and partner. You can't have a great quality of life and a bad relationship with those around you. You can't have great relationships with everyone and a crappy quality of life because they will fill you with hope, love, joy, etc. (the people around you).

There are 2 ways of learning: Either we learn from ourselves through our experiences, our trials, and our mistakes, or from other people who are further along in certain situations that we just entered.

Relationships don't die from lack of love...they die from lack of intimacy. We expect instant gratification from a relationship. The relationship doesn't work that way. It's a place to give, not to take. If you're in a relationship to take, then you turn it into a kind of transaction.

Most of the time we start a relationship with the intention of giving and protecting the other person and then that feeling wears off and we start demanding and feeling a bunch of negative emotions. We turn it over to our ego.

When you started the relationship with what feelings did you enter this relationship? Frustrated, demanding… or grateful, generous, warm, loving…?

If both focus on giving, not taking then this relationship will flourish. But if you start to feel tired, if problems start at work, getting tired from the children, etc. Then we turn it to our ego and what we want for ourselves and forget to give and so the relationship changes for the worse.

We start blaming others. We feel tired, we let the problems get us down, and we blame others for not understanding us, and for asking a lot from us even if they are asking for the same things as before. But because you feel tired and angry and have a bunch of other negative emotions, you change and consider that they demand much more than before. You no longer want to offer as before. You only want to get.

 You don't know how to manage what you experience and how you feel. You don't have the maturity to handle difficulties better. Educate yourself on how to keep your energy and vitality levels high. Train yourself to face difficulties more positively. Don't give up and take for granted in a bad way and neglect your partner, friends, colleagues, etc..

There is a difference in how women and men perceive things.

Women hear words and feel emotions. Non-emotional information is little retained in the woman, and problems are shared as a way of connecting with the partner and others.

Men on the other hand talk nonsense to each other, they don't show emotion. Men generally compartmentalize their emotions to protect themselves from feeling vulnerable. Emotional detachment involves shifting one's focus to a situation and suppressing the emotions that arise. It's when we push hard feelings aside, sweep them under the rug and move on. But these accumulate and turn into outbursts and negative emotions that kill the relationship and the giving as before. They don't communicate, they close in on themselves and they get mad and feel that everything is irritating them.

When a problem arises solve it as fast as you can and if you can't ask for help and if it's something that will be solved in a very slow way and take years then don't get caught up in it focus on other positive events.

Responsibility does not mean burden, but that you can respond, you can actually do something about it. **Responsibility means responding.**

So, think about <u>what role you play in the relationship?</u> Example: The one who always wants to be in control?

What labels and criticism do you put on the other? Example: He's lazy, he doesn't understand me, he's insensitive, etc.

And how does this criticism you make, make you feel? Why do you feel the need to do them? What do you get out of that kind of act?

There can be many reasons why someone may feel the need to criticize others:

1. Personal insecurities: Criticizing others may be a way for some people to feel better about themselves by putting others down.

2. Projection: Sometimes people may criticize others for behaviors or traits that they themselves possess, but are not willing to acknowledge.

3. Power dynamics: In certain situations, such as in a workplace or social hierarchy, people in positions of power may criticize others to assert their dominance or authority.

4. Lack of empathy: Some people may not consider how their words or actions may impact others and may engage in criticism without considering the emotional impact on the recipient.

5. Desire for improvement: In some cases, criticism may be constructive and intended to help the recipient improve in some way.

Why you are doing it?

You can't influence someone positively if you judge them.

And that judgment exists only within our minds. People may not be that bad as we think. What you judge on others is what you don't like about ourselfs.

We are influenced by what we feel about our everyday life and we project it to the other person who does not get rid (for us) of how negative we feel due to how tired we feel as if it is his job. And the other person feels just as tired and projects to us the things he doesn't feel like doing and wants us to do them for him or he is tired of the way we treat him and so with such attitudes, this relationship is doomed.

For a woman to be open to her partner, she must trust and respect him. Love is not enough to have a lively, passionate relationship.

There must be communication from both sides. And don't let things pile up inside you and then you take them out on others.

And try to improve yourself if you see that you: feel tired, bored, you only think about the negatives of everyone. **The problem is with you**. Don't ask the other person to fix how you feel and be angry because they don't do it. **It's your own business to improve yourself not theirs**!

The 3 keys to a relationship are: closeness, closeness, and closeness. Without closeness you don't have chemistry, without chemistry you don't have attraction, without attraction, the mind takes over and frustration, irritation, etc... takes over!

Two qualities without which a relationship cannot exist:

1. **Courage - be willing to open up again.** If you start a relationship by being so cautious that you treat it with malice, and anger, bring out your worst self, and don't express yourself...what do you expect to achieve?

2. **Faith - having the certainty that even when nothing is certain you have faith in something bigger/better.** You don't start a relationship thinking you're going to break up and it won't go well so you don't take it seriously and don't offer yourself.

 Either you will stay in your pain or you will start every relationship with fresh eyes and be there without insecurities and bitterness.

Take responsibility and be honest. And when a relationship brings out the worst in you or you bring out the worst in the other person, walk away. End it!

Get rid of the labels, get rid of the accusations - what and whom you are blaming for every bad thing that has happened to you and is happening to you now- and your story (what you lose, what you don't get,...) and commit to the other person.

Love and relationship are about GIVING and FEELING your partner. Make him/her feel that he/she is the most important thing in your life. Recognize and see the hang-ups and labels and beliefs you place on the other person.

We must make our moments count just as much during those busy days when fatigue is much and not only when we are relaxed.

You need to fill yourself with joy even by taking a bath or a 20-minute walk etc. Try to be your best self every moment. If you come home in a bad mood and this happens often and you don't try to fix how you feel by even being playful, how do you expect the other person to react better?

Think first about how you feel about the other person (whether it's romantic, friendly, professional, or parental) and how you act on them and then accuse him/her of not understanding you or not caring about you. You first project your mood onto the other person and the other person is forced to face it! So, think before you judge and before you put labels on the other person, **in what mood did you come on them?**

To find the root of your relationship problem, ask yourself:

Whose love did you crave the most? Mom's; Dad's or..?

Who were you supposed to be for the people you love? (The good kid? Do as you're told? Take care of Mom's needs? etc.)

 What did you believe? What did they say and what did you think you have to be to be loved?

Who do you respect and love and what are their qualities and characteristic behaviors? And which of their behaviors did you adopt?

Which of their behaviors caused you to adopt some of your own behaviors and reactions, and what are they?

Your decisions are controlled by a set of beliefs that you did not create but were created as automatic coping mechanisms when you were a kid.

Three Top Mistakes Men Make With Women And Women Then Get Introverted, Criticizing, And Disconnecting:

1. **Make her feel like she is invisible:** The women want to radiate... if you pay attention to the changes, she makes on herself and what she offers she will radiate and shine. She needs to be praised and appreciated for what she has to offer.
   So, try saying: Sorry I'm busy now but give me X minutes and I will be with you. Say "I appreciate it....", "You are very beautiful today..."
2. **Make her feel like you don't understand her:** Women want men to understand them even when they don't understand themselves. A woman experiences everything differently, her body, and her emotions. She has the need to share what she feels and thinks and she has the need for a little understanding and compassion in what she is going through and not to judge

her for experiencing it the way she does or to impose a solution on her. **Just being there and being willing to listen**... reduces the intensity with which a woman experiences what she experiences. Women open up because we feel they see us, they recognize us...".

Say something like, "I can't even understand everything you have to deal with or what you're going through, but I'm here and I love you..." Instead of getting angry and thinking of her as a nag. She has different experiences than yours and thinks differently don't forget that.

3.   **Make her feel insecure**: Women generally feel much more at risk than men with what is happening. Instead of feeling calm and connected, when there is a lot of tension it can make women feel somewhat insecure and filled with a lot of strong negative emotions. And then they will either become bossier or want to be in control or they will close in on themselves. If the other person curses her, speaks harshly, derogatorily, badly, hits her, or abuses her, she will feel that she is no longer safe. In general, women need to feel that their partner or brother, or male friends will protect her both physically and emotionally. Women want more presence: presence = feeling connected + CALM!

The 3 mistakes women make towards men:

1.   **You criticize them**: Don't judge them or direct them (don't tell them what to do directly unless they permit you. Do it in a way that is not been seen if you need to do it). Criticism from you is Kryptonian... (as it is on superman). The man wants to be your hero. In other words, he wants you to appreciate him, to admire him, to recognize what he does, to adore him, and to show it to him.

     "Never depend on a man..." can make a man feel "...if you don't have any dependence on me, then why am I here?" Be independent but act like you need his help too. The man grows up thinking that he is someone who serves, inspires, and makes things happen. He likes to please his partner but he also wants to do his own thing. And he wants you to trust him. Men need to learn to handle criticism and not take it so hard.

2.   **Keeping to yourself and not showing emotions**: Men (most) need to open up emotionally and if you make them feel like they can't and that you are a mystery too and they don't know how you feel it "kills" them.

     Men feel, "Let me be who I am...if I'm not good enough, let's move on...I'll change I'll do it better, but on my own terms. If I change because you told me to and I, do it the way you want it, I've lost my center. I also have to maintain who I am."

     Women have tremendous power to make a man more open or closed, but first, they must:

As a woman, there should be a willingness to express deeper truth, to be vulnerable, to go deep beyond the surface...There is always more love but we must open to it on deeper levels. He wants you to extend honesty, kindness, patience, and appreciation.

3. **Control them**: Control and love don't go together. Most women don't even realize they are doing it. They feel so insecure and afraid of men (even dating a man you don't know well is full of all sorts of dangers) and start criticizing, shutting down emotionally, and wanting to control everything out of fear. It is an automatic survival mechanism. **We, women, must also understand that if we relax by giving freedom to the other person and focus on what gives us joy, we will have a more pleasant time.**

Don't forget that for a relationship to work you have to be present and offer. Offering to the other person or they will see that you care about them and listen to his/her needs and he/she will imitate you. Or everything will remain as it is and if that happens that means it's time to break up/stop the friendship, work, etc. And move forward.

Answer the following questions with honesty:

 If you weren't afraid of rejection or getting hurt, what would you do?

What would you be willing to give up to have a relationship full of unlimited love and passion?

What positive and negative qualities/attitudes do you bring to relationships?

Rate with complete honesty how critical you are of others.

And how often do you fall into such behavior (Criticize the other) and what makes you act like that?

How often do you get defensive and what makes you act like that?

How often do you become abrupt and speak condescendingly and arrogantly and what makes you act like that?

How often do you prefer not to talk, ignore the other person and avoid situations and close yourself off and what makes you act like that?

How easy or difficult is it for you to sit down and talk positively with the other person without tension and what makes you act like that?

How easy or difficult is it for you to focus on the other person's positives instead of their negatives and what makes you act like that?

Be aware that if in any relationship the other person is in a state of "**I need help**" it means that they feel that their needs are not being met. And most of the time, this may not even concern you and is simply that their needs remain unsatisfied for so long in their lives. This is why they react with anger, with outbursts because they feel disappointed. It's nothing personal with you and you shouldn't take it that way. What you can do is sit and think if you even want to get involved or even help by satisfying all or some of their needs. And if you can see it as you mature together in this relationship by handling all those behaviors. Without losing who you are and by setting your own limits. Otherwise, leave from the beginning!

Conclusion:

1. When you enter the space where the other person is, you will always greet the other person by name or by their nickname. Depending on what kind of relationship you have.

2. I will always share where I am. Especially with my partner.

3. I will notice and express every change no matter how small on them and express how beautiful they are as a person.

4. I will remind myself that she (or your kid or your friend or..) is different from me so she thinks differently and reacts differently. And instead of telling her how to deal with it by being angry and criticizing her reaction, I'll acknowledge that I admire how she's coping with what she's going through and offer advice with calmness and understanding.

5. I have connected with her a lot, but I almost always lacked to be CALM... Now I know techniques to calm myself down and not cause tension. I know how to help me calm down. I'll take a cold shower or go for a short run, etc. "I feel wonderfully alive when I'm excited, energized, and passionate, and now it's easy for me to calm down so I can be there for my wife, my child, etc..». (use the tips on page 41)

6. Who is responsible for the relationship and who has to work for the relationship? 100% ME! I don't blame the other person for it all the time.

7. Improve yourself so that you have better things to offer in your relationship and everywhere.

8. Sit down and think about what habits make you tired, nervous, angry, etc. And stop doing them. Example: If every time you watch the news you start being upset, stop watching the news.

9. Within us we have masculine and feminine energy. Someone will have more of one than the other. By understanding them we will be able to understand the other person better.

Female, Ying: Focuses on PROCESS and details and every word is a feeling. Issues are reported as a way to connect with others. They are more open people and ready to give and receive love. They want understanding and to be seen not ignored. They stay too long in a relationship and don't leave it easily.

Male, Yang: Words do not translate directly into feelings. Man grows and matures by solving problems. Focus on the RESULT - fight, and not on small details. He is competitive and has difficulty communicating. He doesn't want to feel trapped by life.

10. Everyone wants to feel like the most important thing in their loved one's life when that is violated, it is the fastest way to break up and have resentment. **So just as I need it, so does the other person needs it and I have to show it to them**.

11. When something triggers our malice, anger try saying: "I'm sorry my love (my son..), it's not about you, it triggers me when (do or say- *say what act makes you feel like that)*, you didn't do anything wrong and I don't want to change you is something that makes me feel (say the feeling) and I have to work on it myself and I will...»

12. When a lot of negative things accumulate in our minds because we simply didn't say them when we should, then we start to generalize everything and distort it. This makes us more irritable and less tolerant. We then exaggerate with the slightest. This can also happen when we feel tired all the time and we don't change our program to improve what is causing us so much fatigue. And when you don't say it when you should, then you suddenly burst out and the other person is shocked by your action.

13. Don't look for who started it, who is to blame...!

14. Recognize the labels you put on your partner/friend/child etc. and start removing them!

15. Start focusing on **giving** and let go of the **don't**, that's only in your mind.

16. When we experience something wonderful, we want to share it with someone. When we share it with someone then the beauty of the moment we experience is magnified. That's why having good relationships with people is the most important thing! **That's why the quality of our lives depends on the quality of our relationships with others. They are connected**.

17. People fear 2 things: I'm not good enough and I won't be loved.

18. No relationship was a "failure" and you shouldn't see it that way. Because you learn more about yourself from every relationship. You are filled with valuable life experiences so you always come out victorious. It was an experience from which you learned a lot.

19. When you enter someone's world with compassion and love then that experience will be amazing!

20. In relationships when we exist, we exist either as the person who offers love and understanding or as the person whose every action screams "I need help, save me"»

21. For any relationship to succeed, the values of your purpose and your goals must match. Because if you are not connected and aligned with what your soul longs for, it is incredibly difficult to succeed in your relationships (friendships, working, etc.).

22. What kills relationships are the demands (expectations) we have from others. Change your expectations by appreciating everything the other person offers you and every moment you spend with them.

23. How we behave and what interpretation we give to everything affects how others treat us. It's not just the other person's fault! We must first change how we behave and think and react.

24. It is very different to criticize another person than to simply say what you feel! Break the bad habit of harboring anger and lashing out with criticism because it's easier for you than sitting down and just saying what you feel when you feel it. Start talking by saying "**I feel like**..." and use positive expressions without blaming or criticizing because the other person didn't do what you wanted.

25. Talking and behaving arrogantly, showing disrespect, sarcastic way, cynical way and gesturing do not help! You don't solve anything like that! Instead, do the opposite. Think about the other person's positives and what you appreciated and respect about them when you don't feel angry with them. Think of the positive actions they did and see the positives of the other person through those actions.

26. Being defensive and constantly making excuses for your actions. Blaming others and denying your responsibility and playing the victim doesn't help anywhere. You don't solve anything like that! Change it by accepting the fact that the other person is experiencing it from their perspective and has every right to feel hurt and wronged and just say sorry and make amends. Don't drive him crazy because you want to think you're doing everything perfectly. Because no one is perfect and your perspective is not the only one that exists and it is not the most correct one. The other person is just as correct as your visual side! If something you did hurt him, accept it and make amends, and even if you don't think you hurt him! What matters is that he feels hurt!

27. Closing in on yourself, not paying attention, withdrawing, ignoring the other person, pretending to be busy and generally engaging in self-destructive behaviors don't help anywhere. You don't solve anything like that! Change it and take some time for yourself, engage in activities that calm and soothe you and if you need it, get help from an expert.

28. When you feel angry. Ready to explode. Instead of starting to talk in a way that puts the blame on the other person and that means a fight will start with phrases that start for example "You...", or "I feel like you", it is better to express how you feel so that you can get it out don't let it get exaggerated, but by saying "**I feel furious right now**" and not "<u>You made me furious</u>". Describe what you feel without saying anything else! Start by saying "**I feel...**". Don't start the losing game of blaming the other person because you feel this way. You experience it this way. You interpret it that way. You did not the other person! The other person makes mistakes just like you. He is not infallible. Like you, he experiences a lot of insecurities, and fears that lead him/her to bad and destructive actions and reactions, just like you do. So don't let it overwhelm you. You don't solve anything like that!

29. **To expel or reduce the tension we feel**: We have to RESET for a few minutes: **CHANGE BODY, FOCUS, LANGUAGE**! Change your posture or go out for a walk, focus on something funny or pleasant, or go outside in nature, and as far as 'language' is concerned your words should not be negative and offensive and make laughing faces as silly as you can to calm.

30. You have to start noticing how you react to fights and when you get angry. Only in this way will you be able to see how you behave and to what extent the other person is right when says that you are becoming for example vindictive and trying to improve.

****

When you learn something valuable, try to write it down yourself. Take a pen and paper and write it down. it helps get it out of short-term memory and ingrain it more deeply, and the next time you need to remember it, it will be easier for you to remember.

****

Five keys to sustaining a major change you've just started:

1. **Clarify inside yourself and better write them down, what you really want from life and where you are now**. Clarity is power, the clearer you are about what you want and where you are now, the faster you can achieve things. So be as specific as you can. Think of as many details as you can!

What do you want to achieve?

Why does this excite you?

What it means to you?

Why do you want to achieve it?

When will you achieve it?

How would what you want change the quality of your life and the lives of others?

2. **Crush, destroy, annihilate, and replace any story of containment**. Stop saying, thinking, and focusing on things and events that limit you and fill you with self-pity – sadness, and negativity!! Say "Enough! That's enough! No more! »

 Have you suffered from what?

What you have suffered is not all the events that happened, but it is more your own perception of what happened! Example: You are not depressed because your mother died but because you miss her and want her there by your side. Because you didn't want and you don't want her dead and not because of the event that happened (her death). Try to see the real reason behind the events and the pain you attach to so you can move on!

If you lie to yourself and if you exaggerate you get stuck after that - you get imprisoned. The truth will help you break free. Debunking the facts will set you free.

 So, think again: What are the excuses / limiting beliefs that have kept you from achieving this goal of yours or from maintaining it?

What was your past history that kept you from achieving this goal or any goal of yours?

What is the new story you need to adapt for these new goals of yours?

3. **Notice what kind of language is in what you see and hear and what you say**: In what we see and hear there are words and phrases of hate, fear, anxiety, and all negative emotions. We are emotionally affected by what we see and hear. We are led to focus on fear, hate, etc. **The Brain is like a funnel. The things you see and hear go in and you filter them through your words**. If you say the negative words that you hear and see or if you express yourself afterward just as negatively affected by what negative feeling was instilled in you by what you saw and heard then you need to start paying attention to what you see and hear. <u>What others do is not what will ultimately affect you, but how you react, and how you manage this will.</u> What people do doesn't affect your life, <u>your reactions affect your life!</u> **The words you attach to your every experience become your reality and your story**.

In what we see and hear we are taught that the HOW (how I will do it) is unbearable. Avoid the tyranny of HOW! Keep your enthusiasm, don't let it get lost because you're thinking about how you're going to do it - how it's going to be - how it's going to work. Don't let the **how to** fill you with so much uncertainty that this uncertainty will cause you to **not act** and remain inactive again losing your enthusiasm to try to do what you want / what you thought / your goal.

Beliefs in the style of "If you really get upset, others win", "If you don't stop people they will take advantage of you" all they do is limit you and fill you with hatred, jealousy, malice, etc.

Every time you get angry, irritated, instead of mouthing words that simply feed these feelings, reverse it and think of words and say words that will reduce the intensity with which you feel your anger, etc. **Control your reactions = be aware of your vocabulary**.

4. **Turn uncertainty into action**! If you act strongly, if you act immediately, this is the cure for everything!

Never be idle (without acting) the moment you feel the excitement, or inspiration for something. Immediately make a decision and act on it. Immediately set your goal and act while you are still in the "I promise I will do it" frame of mind. Book a meeting with someone who can help you, buy a relevant book, sign up for specific lessons, or pay someone to guide you.

5. **Give much more than you get**. The secret of life is to give. By giving you will never feel lacking because you add value by giving and you feel full as a human being! You are filled with wonderful feelings that become the driving force afterwards.

We get caught up in the disappointment we feel because we didn't get/weren't offered more or weren't offered what we wanted and lose the meaning of life and joy.

Offer from the little you have and as you get more give more. This way you will stop saying and believing that you don't have this and that because you will see the worst and you will be filled with the love and gratitude you will receive from those you help! You will feel lighter - because you will have lightened from the burden of thinking that you don't have this and the other and from the fear of not having enough! Here's a great goal: to succeed in having more to help more!

****

It is not impossible to change your life for the better! The steps are not that complicated!

I emphasize again: **You must write and think about exactly what you want in every area of your life in detail**! There is no other way!

To see how you have achieved things, think about what you have lived through and think about **how you got here to where you are now?**

How did you manage to overcome so many situations?

What steps did you take back then in each situation and overcome it?

Is there anything you did back then that if you repeat it now will help you?

Consider the following example:

Say you decided to buy a car in a specific brand and white color. Don't you notice that suddenly everywhere you go you see a similar car while before even if it was next to you, you didn't pay attention to it? When you break a leg or an arm or are forced to wear a splint, don't you see people in a similar situation everywhere you go, while before they went unnoticed? So, it is a sample of how much we attract what we experience. And how much we live on autopilot without setting goals and without noticing the beauty around us and life itself! No, it's not beautiful to see others in splints and casts, but think about thinking positively what you'll be seeing more often! Have you ever had to do something you don't want or that you consider too hard as a task and get angry, complain about it, and when you say "no, I'll start with the hard part first, put on music and think I can do it" and devote yourself to do it without negative feelings you see that you do it faster and more correctly? **How we see situations and how we react turn every moment unbearable or easy.**

When we live our day with love without complaining then one thing leads to another and it's as if everything conspires to make our day go smoothly and sometimes full of pleasant little surprises (we meet someone from the past, we find 5 euros on the street, we catch the bus and we don't wait at the bus stop for hours, we find a place to park immediately, etc.).

And if difficulties come but we deal with them in a good mood, then we see the positive that they offered us and we change our opinion on the fact that it was not a bad thing after all (for example we were late getting to the appointment, we couldn't find parking and luckily because we were going to wait there instead of being in our car listening to music or because after all, something else better happened from our delay).

We have to push ourselves to get out of our comfort zone if we want to achieve our goals and if we want to live better. Do not be afraid that you will be disappointed, start! Act!

****

Another mistake we make and we get caught up in misery and negativity:

1. Because in some area of our life, we are not doing well and there are difficulties, we generalize it and think and express ourselves in such a way as if everything is going badly for us when it is not so! For example, you may not have money but you have your health, you are not disabled, and you are not blind. You have good friends while so many people don't have that, etc. Magnifying the situation, all you will achieve is to become ignorant and become the cause of constantly

experiencing bad events because that's what you say, that's what you think, that's what you attract, and then you drown yourself in it!

2. Assuming that the problem is permanent. Saying that no matter what you do it's not going to work. Again, you are condemning yourself. Nothing stays the same forever! Why are you focusing on something so negative and you don't try to react differently « **There is a solution for everything and I will find it! I may not know it now but I will find the solution!** » And keep doing things that fill you with joy and think before you fall asleep « **This is happening in my life (your problem) and I am looking for the most perfect solution! I know it is out there and I will find it!** » Do this for 1-2 months and you will see! Don't let it get you down! Spend at least half an hour every day and imagine how you are untangled, how you found the solution, and <u>see how your life will be because the issue is resolved</u>! **Even if you don't know the solution, see how your life will be because the problem is gone**.

3. Taking every problem as a personal failure and putting negative labels on us. Example "I don't deserve…..I'm not smart enough…..I'm not thin……No! React better! **Do what you love, what makes you laugh!** Take **your attention away** from such thoughts! These thoughts quickly become beliefs and you get yourself limited!

So, think about what wrong beliefs you have about yourself?

What false labels/beliefs need to go?

What is the opposite of the belief that should go?

I can make it!

I can do it!

I can take it to the next level!

I'm amazing!

I'm unstoppable!

I am fearless!

I always succeed!

4. Think about what words you use when you're angry. Okay, now think of humorous words that you can put in place of the words you say when you're angry!

The words you use can give you cheer and strength or make you feel depressed/bad/angry etc.

The words we say and repeat too many times become our beliefs and we end up believing them as our truth. That this is who we are, that this is how our life is. So, get started what are you waiting for? Fix what's holding you back and move forward! Life is waiting for you! Great things await you, let's go!!!

5. Train yourself to act! And the more you do, the stronger you will become psychologically! He who acts will find the solution! It is better to act and take the wrong path because that way you will learn many useful life lessons than not acting! Don't let the flame in you go out! Take action and if that doesn't work, try something else with enthusiasm and positive thinking!

6. **When you feel that you are at your worst, offer help to someone who is worse than you to get out of your negative thoughts! That way you help someone and yourself! Start thinking about what you have with gratitude!**

7. You complain about your job: To see it in a positive way, **think in detail about what would be the worst job in the world for you?** Get started! Say they punish someone and gave them the **worst job in the world how would that look like?**

Do it, you are not here just to read what I write, but to act and do the exercises (answer the questions, write what you need to, and put some of them in your daily routine) otherwise, you will remain the same! Is that what you want?

Now write the opposite about **the best job in the world as you imagine it to be!** Here's your goal! Did you see how easy it was?

8. **So, think about the things you grumble and complain about, write them down, and then write the opposite = write them down in a positive way! And enjoy your goals!**

As hard as you think it is, you have to train yourself to discipline yourself and not allow negative emotions to take root! I have suggested several ways, go try them!

****

And in addition to working and making money, learn to invest wisely and teach your children the same while they are still small so that later they will have a passive income! Strategically invest a small percentage of your salary so that it brings you money even when you sleep!

And when your children grow up, this investment that you taught them to do from a young age has now collected a very big amount for them!

****

So, let's finally make a decision and look at it positively! Life isn't always fair so what can we do!! People are not all good, so what can we do!! We will not give up and we will not pay attention to setbacks! We will say "**There are solutions to everything and we will find them**!" Pain is a part of life, but whether we will suffer and whether we will be imprisoned is up to us! For example, instead of wasting your time saying you don't have money, spend the same time finding a solution! When something disappoints you whether it brings you down or motivates you to do better is up to you!!

All the athletes you brag about spend hours training. They melt during training so you can be happy and proud of the result you see! Have you ever seen how hard they train? Do you see or hear about their personal struggle? No! You only see the end result and not the physical pain, the cramps, the bruises, the lack of time they may have to spend with their loved ones because they are training or if they feel pressured, etc.

If they gave up when they felt tired would they ever get where they did? If they let their phobias, laziness, and boredom take over them and didn't devote all their thought to their goal and to doing the right thing, would they get so far? No!

****

Goal setting is an important process that helps you determine what you want to achieve and create a road map for achieving those goals. Here are some steps to help you set goals:

1. Define your goal: Start by identifying what you want to achieve. This can be a long-term goal or a short-term one. Be specific and clear about what you want to achieve.

2. Make it measurable: A measurable goal is one that you can quantify. This helps you track your progress and know when you've reached your goal. For example, if your goal is to lose weight, set a specific number of pounds that you want to lose rather than staying at the indefinite "I just want to lose weight".

3. Set a deadline: A goal without a deadline is just a dream. Setting a deadline helps you stay focused and motivated. Be realistic and give yourself enough time to reach your goal, but not so much that you lose motivation.

4. Break it down: Break your goal down into smaller, more manageable tasks. This helps you create an action plan and see progress along the way. Each step must be specific, measurable, achievable, relevant, and time-bound.

5. Track Your Progress: Check your progress regularly and adjust your plan if needed. Celebrate your achievements and learn from any setbacks.

6. Goal setting is an essential part of personal and professional development. It helps you create a vision for your future and define the necessary steps to achieve it. It gives meaning to your life.

7. Align your goals with your values: Goals that are aligned with your values are more meaningful and motivating. Take time to think about what is important to you and what you want to achieve.

8. Set both short-term and long-term goals: Short-term goals help you make progress quickly and this will motivate you to keep going, while long-term goals help you create a bigger picture and keep your thinking focused there.

9. Make your goals challenging yet realistic: Goals that are too easy won't motivate you, but goals that are too difficult can lead to frustration and giving up. Find a balance that is challenging but still achievable.

10. Write down your goals: Writing down your goals makes them easier to remember. It also allows you to review them regularly and adjust them as needed.

11. Share your goals with others: Sharing your goals with others can help you stay accountable and get support and encouragement. This can also help you build a network of people who can support you in achieving your goals. Maybe a friend of yours has heard or even knows someone who can help you. If you don't tell him what you want, he won't know it to recommend him to you.

12. Additionally, when writing your goals, it is recommended that you phrase them in a positive way, i.e., **describe what you want to achieve rather than what you don't want to happen**. Examples:

Instead of saying "I don't want to be poorly prepared for the presentation," say "I want to be very well prepared for the presentation".

Instead of saying "I don't want to be late for my work," say "I want to be more efficient and complete my tasks on time ".

13. Visualize success: Visualizing (imagining) success can help you stay excited, motivated and focused on your goals. Take time to imagine how you will feel when you achieve your goals and use that as inspiration to keep going.

14. Remember that setting goals is not something you do and forget about. It is an ongoing process that requires regular review and adjustment. Keep your goals in mind and stay committed to taking action to achieve them.

Below are some examples of different types of goals:

Career Goals: What you could have written: Get a promotion within the next year. Attend a professional development seminar or conference. Completion of a certification or degree program to improve skills and qualifications. Then you write them again in details and with the actions you will take.

Financial goals: Save $10,000 for a down payment on a home. Pay off your credit card debt within the next 12 months. Start a retirement account and contribute a certain amount each month (you write how much). Then you write them again in details and with the actions you will take

Health and wellness goals: I will exercise for 30 minutes a day, five days a week. I will lose 20 kilos by the end of the year. I will quit smoking by (a specific date). Then you write them again in details and with the actions you will take.

Personal development goals: I will learn a new skill, such as a language or a musical instrument. I will read one book a month for the next year. I will volunteer for a cause I care about and go regularly. Then you write them again in details and with the actions you will take.

Relationship Goals: Spend more quality time with family and friends each week. Improve communication in your romantic relationship by attending counseling sessions or reading books on the subject. Reconnect with a friend or family member you've lost touch with.

1. Remember, when making goals, it is important that they are specific with details, measurable, achievable, relevant and time-bound (Smart Goals). By doing this, you can break each goal down into actionable steps and track your progress.
2. Focus on the "why": Before setting a goal, take time to think about why it's important to you. Understanding the underlying motivation for your goal will help you stay committed and motivated, even when there are obstacles.
3. Be realistic: While it's important to set ambitious goals, it's also important to be realistic. Setting goals that are too far from your level can lead to frustration and discouragement. Instead, set goals that are challenging yet achievable.
4. Use positive language: When setting goals, use positive language to frame them. Instead of saying, "I want to stop eating fattening foods," say, "I'm going to start eating healthier foods." This can help you create a more positive mindset and keep you inspired and excited about your goal.
5. Make a plan: After setting your goals, create a plan to achieve them. Break each goal down into smaller, easier steps and create a timeline for completing each section. This can help you stay focused and stay on track.
6. Track Your Progress: Track your progress toward your goals regularly. This can help you stay focused on your goals and make the necessary adjustments. You

can use a calendar, a whiteboard (Place it somewhere you can see it all the time.), or a goal tracking app to record your progress.

Staying motivated is often a key challenge when it comes to achieving goals. Here are some strategies that can help:

1. Use positive self-talk (what you say to yourself): Negative self-talk can be discouraging and undermine your confidence. Try to replace negative thoughts with positive affirmations and **focus on your strengths and achievements**.

2. Build a support network: Having a supportive network of family, friends or colleagues who can offer encouragement and advice can be helpful. You can also consider joining a support group or hiring a mentor or coach to help you stay focused on your goals and motivated.

3. Celebrate successes: **Celebrating small successes along the way** can be a great motivator. Take time to celebrate and reward yourself. Celebration can help keep your motivation and energy (aliveness, enthusiasm) high.

4. Visualize Success: Take time to **visualize yourself achieving your goals**. Imagine the feeling of accomplishment and success you will experience. Think about how you live the way you want! You have the freedom to do everything you want! How do you feel; How is your life now? What feelings arise in you because you wake up every day having everything you want? This can help you stay focused and motivated.

5. Focus on the benefits: **Remind yourself of the benefits that achieving your goals will bring.** Whether it's improved health, financial stability or personal growth. Keeping the benefits in mind can help keep you motivated and not give up by any setbacks and delays.

6. Remember, staying motivated is a process that requires constant effort and dedication. By using these strategies and maintaining a positive mindset, you can stay motivated about your goals and achieve the success you desire.

7. Track Your Progress: Regularly tracking your progress can help you stay motivated. This can be as simple as checking off completed steps on a step list (written on paper or on the computer or on a whiteboard somewhere at home) or using a habit tracking app (on your phone or tablet) to keep track your progress. Seeing your progress can help you stay motivated and build momentum. Check all the steps you took, change the ones that don't fit anymore, mark your victories and what helped you reach a small or big victory, etc.

8. Be kind to yourself: Remember that setbacks and failures are a natural part of the process. Don't get mad at yourself if you get off track. Instead, practice self-

compassion and remind yourself that failures are an opportunity to learn and grow. **A new acquaintance, a new idea can arise from a failure**.

9. Focus on the process, not just the outcome: While it's important to have a clear outcome in mind, focusing solely on the end result can be overwhelming. Instead, focus on the daily habits and actions that will help you achieve your goal. Celebrate small wins along the way and stay committed to the process.

10. Be inspired: **Surround yourself with** people and **resources that inspire you**. Whether listening to seminars and videos on how to find motivation - setting goals or reading inspirational biographies and books on such topics. Immersing yourself in success stories can help you stay motivated and filled with energy and enthusiasm.

11. Reexamine your why: Finally, if you find your motivation waning, take a moment to **rethink why you set your goal in the first place**. Reconnecting with your underlying motivation can help rekindle your passion and keep you focused on your desired outcome.

****

How to find your potential customers. How to learn more about their needs and the tools you will need. Below are some strategies you can use:

1. Conduct market research: Market research involves gathering information about your target audience, including their demographics, interests, and buying behavior. This can be done through surveys, focus groups or online research. You can also use market research companies to conduct in-depth studies.

2. Analyze existing customer data: If you have an existing customer base, analyzing their data can provide insight into who is buying your products. You can view data such as age, location, gender and purchase history to spot trends and patterns.

3. Attending your industry events and trade shows can provide an opportunity to connect with potential customers and learn more about their interests and needs.

4. Working with influencers in your industry can help you reach a wider audience and gain insights into the interests and buying behaviors of their followers.

5. Conduct surveys: Surveys are a simple and effective way to gather information about your target audience. You can create a survey using free online tools like Google Forms or SurveyMonkey and then share it with your email list or social media followers. Be sure to ask questions that will provide insight into your

customers' needs and interests. Create gallop - poll questions and answers to find out what your audience is asking for, what complaints they have, what improvements to make.

6. Market Test Your Product: Market testing your product can help you better understand your target audience. You can use customer feedback to improve your product and gain insight into who is buying it.

7. Remember, understanding your target market is an ongoing process that requires consistent effort and research. Using these strategies, you can gain valuable insights into your potential customers and improve your marketing efforts to better meet their needs.

8. Conduct online research: Use search engines and social media platforms to research your industry, competitors and potential customers. You can search for forums, groups and discussions related to your product or service to gain insight into the interests and needs of your target market.

9. When your product is ready put the questionnaire inside and tell your customers to fill it out and send it to you or tell them on which page they can go and do your poll and they will get a gift if they do your poll and tell them what kind of gift it will be.

10. Use Google Trends: Google Trends is a free tool that provides information on search volume and trends related to specific keywords or topics. You can use this tool to spot trends and patterns related to your industry or product.

11. Use social media analytics: Many social media platforms provide free analytics tools that allow you to analyze your audience and their behaviors. For example, on Facebook, you can use the Page Insights tool to analyze the demographics and behaviors of your followers.

12. Remember, while paid market research services can provide more detailed and comprehensive information, there are many free resources available to help you better understand your target market. By using these resources and staying engaged in the process, you can gain valuable insights into your potential customers and improve your marketing efforts to better meet their needs.

13. Join Online Communities: Online communities like forums and social media groups can be a great source of information about your target market. Joining these communities and participating in discussions can help you better understand your customers' problems, interests, and behaviors.

14. Analyze your customer reviews: Online customer reviews can provide valuable insight into the experiences and opinions of your target market. Look for

patterns and trends in reviews to identify areas for improvement and better understand your customers' needs.

15. Do Keyword Research: Keyword research involves identifying the search terms and phrases your potential customers use to find products or services like yours. You can use free tools like Google Keyword Planner to conduct keyword research and gain insight into the interests and needs of your target market.

16. Take Free Webinars: Many businesses and organizations offer free webinars related to specific industries or topics. Attending these webinars can provide an opportunity to learn from industry experts and connect with potential clients.

****

Improving as a person is an ongoing journey that involves personal growth, learning and self-reflection. Here are some strategies to help you improve as a person:

1. **Set goals**: Setting specific, achievable goals can help you focus your efforts and track your progress over time. Identify areas in your life where you would like to improve, such as your career, relationships or health, and set goals that align with your values and priorities.

2. **Practice self-care**: Taking care of your physical, emotional and mental well-being is essential to personal growth. Make time for activities that promote relaxation and reduce stress, such as exercise, meditation, or spending time in nature.

3. **Learn new skills**: Learning new skills can help you expand your knowledge and improve your abilities. Consider taking a class, attending a workshop, or reading books on topics that interest you.

4. **Seek feedback**: Seeking feedback from others can provide valuable insight into your strengths and areas for improvement. Ask friends, family or colleagues for constructive feedback and be open to their suggestions.

5. **Engage in self-reflection**: Regularly reflecting on your thoughts, feelings, and behaviors can help you better understand yourself and make positive changes. Consider keeping a journal or taking time to reflect on your day or week depending on how easily you forget.

6. **Practice Gratitude**: Cultivating a sense of gratitude can help you appreciate the positive aspects of your life and cultivate a more positive outlook and attitude towards life. Make it a habit to think about the things you are grateful for every day.

7. **Help others**: Helping others can provide a sense of purpose and fulfillment. Consider volunteering in your community or taking time to support friends or family members in need.
8. **Don't forget, improving as a person** is a personal journey that requires commitment and effort. By using these strategies and staying open to growth and learning, you can become a better version of yourself and live a more fulfilling life.
9. **Embrace change**: Change is an inevitable part of life and embracing it can help you grow and evolve as a person. Be open to new experiences and opportunities and be willing to take risks and try new things.
10. **Surround yourself with positive influences**: The people you surround yourself with can have a significant impact on your personal growth. Seek out relationships and social circles that support your goals and encourage you to be the best version of yourself.
11. **Practice self-compassion**: It's important to be kind and compassionate to yourself, even when you make mistakes or face setbacks. Practice self-compassion by treating yourself with the same kindness and understanding you would extend to a friend.
12. **Write yourself a letter of advice and compassion** as if you were writing it to a friend who needs you and is going through the same thing as you. Think about what advice you would give your friend.
13. **Develop a Growth Mindset and Positive Thinking**: A growth mindset involves viewing challenges and failures as opportunities to learn and grow. Focus on the process of learning and improvement, rather than the outcome, and celebrate your progress even the smallest daily achievements (who did you help today, what went well today, what made you feel good today even for a minute, what made you smile, these are also a type of daily gratitude) .
14. **Take responsibility for your life**: Taking responsibility for your thoughts, feelings and actions can help you feel more in control of your life and empowered to make positive changes. Instead of blaming others or external circumstances for your problems, focus on what you can do to take action and create positive change.
15. **Engage in meaningful activities**: Engaging in activities that align with your values and bring your sense of purpose can help you feel more fulfilled and happier with your life. Consider pursuing hobbies, volunteering, or participating in other activities that bring you joy and give meaning to your life.

16. **Build strong relationships**: Building and maintaining positive relationships with others can be a key factor in your personal growth. Cultivate meaningful connections with friends, family and colleagues through open communication, empathy and mutual respect.

17. **Practice mindfulness**: Mindfulness involves being fully present in the moment (the now), without judgment or distraction. Regularly practicing mindfulness techniques such as meditation or deep breathing can help reduce stress, increase self-awareness and improve your overall well-being.

18. **Notice everything around you**. When you walk to go to the bakery or to work or to the market, look around you at everything. Don't walk on autopilot without noticing the beauty of life, the sun, the people, etc. Get out and watch the sunset and the sun rise in the morning. Plant 2-3 pots and admire the beauty of your flowers. Go to an animal shelter and pet the animals, hug them, fill them with love.

19. **Constantly learn and educate yourself**: Learning new things is essential for personal growth and development. Take advantage of opportunities to learn new skills, attend workshops or seminars and read books on topics that interest you.

20. **Practice empathy**: Empathy involves putting yourself in someone else's shoes and trying to understand their perspective. Practicing empathy can help you improve your relationship and communication skills, as well as increase your understanding of others and their experiences.

21. **Take care of your physical health**: Your physical health can have a significant impact on your overall well-being and personal growth. Make sure you eat a balanced diet, exercise regularly and take care of any health concerns or problems that arise.

22. **Practice good time management**: Time management skills can help you prioritize your goals and use your time more efficiently. Set realistic deadlines, create a schedule or to-do list, and focus on completing tasks that are most important or urgent.

23. **Embrace failure as a learning opportunity**: Failure is a natural part of the learning process and can be an opportunity for growth and development. Instead of being discouraged by failure, use it as an opportunity to learn and improve.

****

Staying positive can be challenging, especially when faced with stress and adversity. However, there are many simple things you can do in your daily life to maintain a positive outlook. Here are some ideas:

1. **Practice Gratitude:** Take time each day to think about what things you are grateful for in your life. This can help shift your focus from the negative to the positive and help you appreciate what you have. Keep a gratitude journal: Write down **three things you are grateful for each day** in a journal. This can help you **focus on the positive aspects of your life** and **appreciate the good things happening around you**.
2. **Surround yourself with positivity**: Surround yourself with positive people and influences and **avoid those who bring negativity into your life**. This can include spending time with supportive friends and family members who are positive people and enjoy being with them. Listen to uplifting music and read positive literature and books on positive thinking. See similar videos too.
3. **Take care of your physical health**: Taking care of your physical health can have a significant impact on your mental well-being. Make sure you eat a balanced diet, exercise regularly and prioritize getting enough sleep.
4. **Engage in activities that bring you joy**: Engaging in activities that bring you joy can help boost your mood and stay positive. This can include hobbies, spending time in nature, or volunteering for a cause you believe in.
5. **Practice Mindfulness**: Practicing mindfulness can help you stay present in the moment and reduce stress and anxiety. You can practice mindfulness through meditation, breathing exercises, or simply focusing on your surroundings.
6. **Laugh and have fun**: Laughter can be a powerful tool for reducing stress and promoting positivity. **Find time to have fun**, either by watching a funny movie or spending time with friends who make you laugh or watch funny videos.
7. **Practice self-compassion**: Treat yourself with kindness and compassion, especially when you're going through a tough time. **Avoid negative self-talk** and be kind to yourself as you would to a close friend. **Practice positive self-talk**: The **way we talk to ourselves can have a significant impact on our mood and outlook**. Try to replace negative self-talk with more positive affirmations and statements and focus on your strengths and achievements.
8. **Connect with others**: Make an effort to connect with others regularly, whether through a hobby group, volunteer work, or simply spending time with friends and family.

9. **Learn to manage stress**: Stress can take a toll on our mental and physical health, so it's important to have strategies to manage it. This may include regular exercise, relaxation techniques such as meditation or deep breathing, or engaging in activities that help you feel calm and centered.
10. **Cultivate a growth mindset**: Embrace challenges as opportunities for growth and learning, rather than obstacles. A growth mindset can help you stay optimistic and focused on possibilities, even when you face difficulties.
11. **Take breaks and prioritize rest**: It's important to prioritize rest and relaxation in your daily routine, especially if you're feeling overworked or stressed. Taking regular breaks can help you recharge and feel more positive and energized.
12. **Focus on solutions, not problems**: When faced with a challenge or difficulty, try to focus on finding a solution instead of focusing on the problem. This can help you **feel more empowered and in control**, and can help you stay positive even in the face of adversity.
13. **Use positive affirmations**: Repeat positive affirmations to yourself regularly, such as "**I am capable,**" "**I am worthy,**" or "**I am strong.**" This can **help boost your confidence and self-esteem** and help you stay positive and motivated.
14. **Engage in acts of kindness**: Doing something nice for someone else can help boost your mood and promote positive feelings. This can be as simple as offering a compliment, holding the door for someone, or helping someone in need.
15. **Practice self-care**: Make time for activities that help you feel refreshed and rejuvenated, such as taking a bubble bath, getting a massage, or spending time in nature. Taking care of yourself can help you feel more positive and energetic.
16. **Seek support when needed**: Don't hesitate to reach out to friends, family or professionals if you're feeling overwhelmed or struggling with negative thoughts. Seeking support can help you feel less alone and give you the resources you need to stay positive and resilient.
17. Remember, staying positive is a process and it takes practice and patience to cultivate a more positive outlook.

****

To help you figure out what kind of great deal to offer your customers and how, you can try the following strategies. By implementing these strategies, you can offer an amazing deal to your customers and stand out from your competitors.

1. To offer a great deal, **you need to understand your customers' needs** and preferences. Conduct market research to determine what your customers want and use this information to create an offer that aligns with their interests.

2. **Create a sense of urgency**: People are more likely to take action when they feel something is urgent. **Offer offers that are only available for a short time to create a sense of urgency and encourage customers to act quickly**. Consider using language that states the offer is for a limited time only or that supplies are limited.

3. **Bundle products or services**: Bundle products or services together to offer a more complete solution to your customers' needs. For example, you could offer a bundle that includes several products or services at a very discounted price.

4. **Offer a free trial or sample**: People are more likely to buy something when they've had a chance to try it. Offer a free trial or sample of your product or service to let customers experience it for themselves. And why not reward them with something free to rate their experience so you can learn the pros and cons of what you offered to improve it!

5. **Personalize the offer**: Personalization can make customers feel valued and special. Use data and insights to personalize your offers to customers based on their past purchases, browsing history or other preferences.

6. **Make sure your offer is easy to understand and redeem**. Avoid complicated terms and conditions and make the process of redeeming the offer simple and with clear easy-to-read few terms.

7. **Providing excellent customer service** can go a long way in building customer loyalty and satisfaction. Ensure you have a process in place to handle customer queries, complaints and feedback in a timely and professional manner.

8. **Make the offer valuable**: The more value you can offer your customers, the more likely they are to take advantage of the offer. Consider offering a discount, free gift, or free service that is of great value to your customers.

9. **Make the offer exclusive**: People like to feel like they are getting something special. Create an offer that is exclusive to a specific group of customers, such as loyal customers, new customers or customers who refer friends.

10. **Use social proof**: Social proof is a powerful marketing tool that can help convince customers to take action. Use testimonials, reviews or case studies to prove the value of your offering and show that other customers have had positive experiences with your product or service.

11. **Create a sense of anticipation**: Create excitement and anticipation around your offer by promoting it on your website, social media channels or in your email newsletter. Use attention-grabbing headlines and graphics to generate buzz and generate interest in the offer.

12. **Make the offer easy to share**: Encourage your customers to share the offer with their friends and family by making it easy to share on social media or via email. Offer a referral bonus or incentive for customers who refer others to your business.

13. **Analyze the results**: Once you've launched your promotion, monitor the results to see how it's performing. Use analytics and customer feedback to learn what's working and what could be improved, and use this information to improve your future offerings.

14. Remember, creating an amazing offer is only one part of the overall customer experience. Make sure you provide a high-quality product or service and provide excellent customer service to back up your offering. By providing value, exclusivity, social proof, anticipation, shareability and analytics, you can create an offering that your customers will love and help your business grow.

15. **Place your offer at the right time** and moment depending on what you are offering: Timing is everything when it comes to creating an amazing offer. Consider starting your offer at a time when your customers are most likely to buy, such as during the holiday or back-to-school season.

16. **Segment your audience**: Not all customers are the same. Consider segmenting your audience based on factors such as age, location or purchasing habits to create offers tailored to each segment (for each type of customer).

17. **Use visual aids**: People are visual creatures, so consider using visual aids such as videos, images or charts to promote your offer. This can help them remember it and make your offer memorable.

18. **Provide clear instructions**: Make sure your customers know exactly what they need to do to take advantage of your offer. Provide clear instructions on how to redeem the offer and any associated terms and conditions. And don't make it complicated!

19. **Use a sense of humor**: If it's appropriate for your brand, consider adding some humor to your offer. This can help make your brand more trustworthy and memorable and can create positive associations with your business.

20. **Follow up with customers**: After a customer takes advantage of your offer, follow up with them to see if they liked your product or service. This can help you build a stronger relationship with your customers and encourage repeat business.

21. Creating an amazing offer can be a great way to attract new customers, build loyalty and increase sales. By considering factors such as timing, segmentation,

graphics, instructions, humor and continuity, you can create an offer that stands out and creates positive associations with your brand.

22. **Offer a risk-free trial**: Customers may be more willing to try your product or service if they know they can do so risk-free. Consider offering a money-back guarantee or free trial to encourage customers to take the plunge.

23. **Make the offer easy to understand**: Make sure your offer is easy to understand and communicate. Use simple language and make sure the offer is easy to find and access on your website or other marketing materials.

24. **Partner with other businesses**: Consider partnering with other businesses that complement your products or services to create a joint offering. This can help you reach new audiences and provide more value to your customers.

25. **Giving gifts to your customers** can be a great way to show your appreciation, build loyalty and encourage repeat business.

Here are some gift ideas you can give your customers:

1. **Items with your brand on them**: Branded merchandise such as t-shirts, hats or mugs can be a great way to promote your brand and give your customers something tangible to remember you by.

2. **Samples of your products or services**: If you offer a product or service, consider giving samples to your customers. This can help them try your products or services without committing to a purchase and can encourage them to make a purchase in the future.

3. **Handwritten Notes**: A handwritten note is a thoughtful and personal way to show your appreciation to your customers. Consider writing a note to thank them for their purchase and express your gratitude for their support. And why not add some humor.

4. **Gift cards** are a great way to give your customers something they can use to make a purchase from your business or a partner business.

5. **Give them something they ask for a lot in small doses** or in miniature with the brand on it.

6. **Offering discounts on future purchases** can be a great way to encourage repeat purchases and show your appreciation to your customers. Give a very big discount for the first purchase or if they buy a specific amount.

7. **Donations to charity**: Consider making a donation to charity on your client's behalf. This can be a meaningful way to show your appreciation and support a cause that is important to your customer.

8. **Plant a tree** in your client's name.

9. **Offer him something that is good for the planet**. Something ecological and useful as well.
10. **Offer free entry to self-improvement seminars**.
11. Remember to choose a gift that is right for your brand and your customers. Consider your budget, your brand image, and your customers' preferences and needs when choosing a gift.
12. **Custom Gifts**: Consider creating diaries, notebooks or phone cases with your brand or personalized message. These items can be practical and useful for your customers in their daily life.
13. Give them a **book** as a gift.
14. **Offer as a gift 30-day** fitness or yoga membership or psychotherapy, from someone you'll partner with for mutual advertising.
15. **E-books or guides**: If you are in the business of providing knowledge or expertise, consider giving your customers an e-book or guide related to your industry. This can help position your business as a thought leader and deliver value to your customers.
16. **Food or drinks**: Offering food or drinks can be a great way to create an unforgettable experience for your customers. This could include a basket of fresh fruit, a box of chocolates or a packet of gourmet coffee or tea.
17. **Digital products**: If you have digital products, such as software or online courses, consider giving your customers access to them as a gift. This can provide value to your customers and help them get the most out of your products or services.
18. **VIP Experiences**: For your most loyal or high-value customers, consider offering a VIP experience, such as an invitation to a special event or access to exclusive content or product. This can help you build a strong relationship with your customers and make them feel valued.
19. Consider giving your customers **personalized gifts**, such as a monogrammed journal, engraved pen or frame. These items can make your customers feel special and appreciated.
20. **Subscription Boxes**: Offering a subscription box service can be a great way to provide ongoing value to your customers. Consider curating a box of products related to your industry or offering a personalized subscription service tailored to your customers' needs.
21. **Practical items**: Consider giving your customers practical items that they can use in their daily lives. This can include items such as phone chargers, portable batteries or reusable shopping bags.

22. **Event tickets**: Consider giving your customers tickets to a concert, sporting event or theater performance. This can provide an unforgettable experience and help build a strong relationship with your customers.
23. **Free services**: Consider offering a free service or consultation to your customers as a gift. This can help you demonstrate the value of your products or services and provide a positive experience for your customers.
24. Give a free ticket to the first 5 people that will buy to an event that is very great and popular.

****

Providing excellent customer service is vital for any business as it can create loyal customers, improve the company's reputation and ultimately increase sales. **Here are some tips on how to provide excellent customer service, along with some examples**:

1. **Listen to customers**: One of the most important aspects of providing excellent customer service is listening to your customers. You should actively listen to their concerns and needs and then address them appropriately. Some examples of how to listen actively include asking open-ended questions and reflecting on what the customer has said to ensure you understand their concerns. If a customer is unhappy with a product, listen to their concerns, ask questions about the problems they're having, and work with them to find a solution. If a customer is having trouble using a product, actively listen to their concerns, ask them to describe the problems they're having, and then offer a solution or help.
2. **Respond quickly**: Customers expect quick responses, whether it's via social media, email or phone. This allows customers to contact you in the most convenient way for them. Responding to customers quickly shows that you care about their concerns and take them seriously. For example, a company that provides 24/7 customer service through various channels such as chat, email, and phone can respond to customer inquiries within minutes or hours, depending on the urgency.
3. **Be empathetic**: Empathy means putting yourself in the customer's shoes and understanding their perspective. This can be achieved by acknowledging the customer's feelings and showing genuine interest. For example, if a customer is unhappy with a product or service, a company can offer a sincere apology and assure the customer that it will do everything it can to make things right. If a customer is unhappy with a product, acknowledge their frustration and apologize for any inconvenience. If a customer has a problem with a service,

show them that you understand their frustration and that you take their concerns seriously.

4. **Provide solutions**: Customers want solutions to their problems, not just an apology and that was it. Therefore, it is essential to provide customers with practical solutions to their problems. For example, a company could offer a refund, exchange, or free product to make up for a mistake or bad experience.

5. **Go above and beyond**: To create a lasting very good impression, a company should go above and beyond to meet the customer's needs. This can be done by offering personalized service or by providing something extra to make the customer experience memorable. For example, a restaurant could offer a free dessert to a customer celebrating their birthday, or a retailer could offer free shipping on a customer's next purchase. If a customer waits a long time, offer a free drink or snack or something related to what you offer.

6. **Train and empower employees**: Finally, it is important to train and empower employees to provide excellent customer service. This means giving employees the necessary tools, resources and authority to solve customer problems quickly and efficiently. Additionally, employees should be trained to communicate effectively, handle difficult customers, and provide personalized service (There are so many training courses you could pay for and provide for free to your staff). Examples: Provide employees with customer service training that includes effective communication, active listening, and conflict resolution. Empower employees to make decisions that benefit the customer, such as providing a discount or free product.

7. And don't forget an employee who feels good in the place he works and doesn't feel wronged will provide very good service on his own because he respects and values his boss and his work.

****

Social media can be a powerful tool for promoting your work and building your personal brand. **Here are some tips for using social media to promote your work and yourself:**

1. **Choose the right platforms**: There are a variety of social media platforms available, each with their own strengths and weaknesses. Consider which platforms are most popular among your target audience and which best suit your goals.

2. **Be consistent**: Posting content regularly on social media is key to building a strong presence and engaging with your audience. Consider creating a content calendar to make sure you're posting regularly.

3. **Use visual content**: Visual content such as images and videos are more likely to grab people's attention on social media than text alone. Consider creating visual content that is both informative and engaging.

4. **Engage with your audience**: social media is a two-way conversation. Be sure to respond to comments and messages from your audience and interact with other people's content by liking, commenting and sharing.

5. **Use hashtags**: Hashtags can help your content reach a wider audience by making it easier for people to find your content. Research popular hashtags related to your industry or topic and use them in your posts. (Hashtags are words or phrases preceded by the "#" symbol, used to categorize and group social media content. Hashtags first became popular on Twitter, but are now used on many other social media platforms, such as Instagram, Facebook, LinkedIn and Tik Tok.

   Using hashtags allows users to easily discover content related to a specific topic. By clicking on a hashtag, users can see all posts that include that tag, regardless of who posted them or when they were posted. This feature allows users to discover new content, follow conversations and interact with people who share similar interests.

   Hashtags can be created for any topic, from broad concepts like #travel, to specific events like #SuperBowl. Here are some examples of how hashtags are used on different social media platforms:

   Twitter: Twitter was the first platform to introduce hashtags and they are still widely used on the site. Users often add hashtags to their tweets to make them more discoverable. For example, a user can tweet "I love this new #book I just read! #bookreview #amreading" to connect with other book lovers and share their thoughts on a particular book.

   Instagram: Instagram is a highly visual platform and hashtags are an important way for users to discover new content related to their interests. Hashtags on Instagram are often used to describe the content of the post, such as #foodie or #travelgram. They can also be used to add a branded element to the post, such as #Nike or #CocaCola.

   Facebook: Facebook introduced hashtags in 2013 and they are now commonly used on the platform. Hashtags on Facebook are similar to those on Instagram and are often used to categorize content and make it more discoverable. For example, a user can share a post about their workout routine and add hashtags like #fitness, #motivation, and #workouttips.

   TikTok: TikTok is a video sharing platform that has become extremely popular in recent years. Hashtags on TikTok are used to categorize and discover videos related to specific topics, such as #dancechallenge or #travelvibes. Users can add hashtags to their videos to make them more discoverable and connect with others interested in similar content.

6. **Share your expertise**: social media is a great platform to share your expertise and build your personal brand. Consider sharing your ideas and opinions on your industry or topic and providing value to your audience.

7. **Use Paid Advertising**: Consider using paid advertising on social media to reach a larger audience. This may include options such as promoted posts, sponsored content, or pay-per-click advertising.

8. **Collaborate with others**: Collaborating with other professionals or social media influencers can help you reach a wider audience and make new connections. Consider working with others in your industry or niche for co-promotions or partnerships.

9. **Be authentic**: Authenticity is key when building a personal brand on social media. Be yourself and share your personal story to create a connection with your audience.

10. **Provide value**: Provide valuable content to your social media audience by sharing your experience, offering advice, or sharing helpful resources. This can help you build trust with your audience and position yourself as an authority in your field.

11. **Monitor your analytics**: Use social media analytics to track the performance of your content and make adjustments as needed. This can help you understand what works and what doesn't and improve your social media strategy over time.

12. Remember that social media is only one aspect of your overall marketing strategy. Consider using a variety of tactics to promote your work and yourself, including email marketing, networking events, and public speaking engagements. By leveraging a variety of marketing channels, you can reach a wider audience and build your personal brand over time.

13. **Use of media**: Experiment with a variety of media formats to keep your content fresh and engaging. Consider using live videos, infographics, podcasts or other types of media to share your message and reach your audience.

14. **Use tools to alert you when someone writes about you**: Use social media monitoring tools to track what people are saying about you or your brand online. This can help you identify opportunities to engage with your audience, respond to customer complaints and address any negative feedback.

15. **Leverage user-generated content**: Encourage your followers to create and share content related to your brand or products. This can help you reach a wider audience and create a sense of community around your brand.

16. **Stay up to date with the latest trends** and changes on social media platforms to ensure your content is relevant and effective. Follow experts on social media, attend industry events and participate in online forums and communities to stay up-to-date with the latest best practices.

17. **Engage with influencers**: Connect with influencers in your industry or niche on social media and engage with their content. Leave comments, share their posts and mention them in your own content. This can help you build relationships with key influencers and expand your reach.

18. **Optimize your social media profiles** by including a professional headshot or logo, a compelling bio, and links to your website or other relevant online properties. This can help you make a strong first impression and encourage people to follow or engage with you.

19. **Provide social proof**: Use social proof to demonstrate your credibility and expertise. This may include sharing testimonials from satisfied customers, showing off your awards or certifications, or sharing examples of your work or projects.

20. **Engage with your audience**: Engage with your audience on social media by asking questions, responding to comments and hosting live Q&A sessions. This can help you build relationships with your followers and showcase your expertise.

21. Remember that social media is a tool. It takes time and effort to build a strong social media presence, so be patient and persistent in your efforts.

****

Choosing the right social media platform can be a daunting situation, especially when there are so many options available. Each platform has its own unique characteristics and audience. To determine which social media platform is best for your needs, it is necessary to consider your goals, target audience and type of content. **Here's a rundown of the most popular social media platforms and their strengths and weaknesses.**

1. **Facebook** is the largest social networking platform, with over 2.8 billion active users. It is suitable for businesses and individuals who want to reach a wide audience. The platform allows you to create a business page, share updates, photos and videos with your followers and interact with them through

comments, likes and shares. However, due to its size and popularity, it can be difficult to distinguish and reach your target audience.

Advantages:

• It has a huge user base, which makes it a great platform for businesses and individuals who want to reach a wide audience.

• Offers a range of advertising options, including targeting options, to help businesses reach their ideal audience.

• Supports a range of content formats including photos, videos and live videos, making it a versatile platform.

Disadvantages:

• It can be difficult to reach your target audience organically due to the size of the platform and the amount of content shared daily.

• It can be time consuming to create content for the platform and the algorithm can be unpredictable at times.

• There are concerns about the privacy and security of data on the platform, which may affect user trust.

Examples of successful Facebook pages: Coca-Cola, Oreo and Red Bull.

2. **Instagram** is a visual platform that allows users to share photos and videos with their followers. It is suitable for businesses and individuals who want to present their products or services visually. The platform also offers a range of features such as stories, reels (one-minute-only videos) and IGTV to help you connect with your followers and reach new audiences.

Advantages:

• It is a visual platform, making it ideal for businesses and individuals who want to present their products or services visually.

• Offers a range of features including stories, reels and IGTV to help you connect with your followers and reach new audiences.

• It is popular among the younger demographic, making it a great platform for businesses targeting this age group.

Disadvantages:

• It is primarily a mobile app, which can make managing content from a desktop computer difficult.

• It can be difficult to get your content seen organically, especially if you have a small following.

• There are concerns about Instagram's impact on mental health due to its focus on visual perfection.

Examples of successful Instagram pages: National Geographic, Nike and Glossier.

3. **Twitter** is a microblogging platform that allows users to share short updates, called tweets, with their followers. It is suitable for businesses and individuals who want to share news, updates and quick thoughts with their audience. The platform also allows for real-time interaction with followers through replies and retweets.

   Advantages:
   - It is a great platform to share quick updates and interact with followers in real time.
   - It is popular among journalists and leaders, making it a great platform for businesses and individuals who want to establish themselves as experts in their field.
   - It is easy to use and requires minimal effort to create content.

   Disadvantages:
   - It is primarily a text-based platform, which can make sharing visual content difficult.
   - The character limit (currently 280 characters) may be restrictive for some users who want to share more in-depth content.
   - The platform moves quickly and tweets can quickly get lost in such a huge volume of posts.
   - It can be difficult to gain a significant following organically, especially if you are starting out.

   Examples of successful Twitter pages: Elon Musk, Wendy's and The New York Times.

4. **LinkedIn** is a social media platform primarily focused on professional networking. It is suitable for businesses and individuals who want to connect with other professionals in their industry, share industry news and updates, and showcase their professional skills and experience. The platform also offers advertising and recruitment solutions for businesses.

   Advantages:
   - It is a great platform for professional networking and connecting with other professionals in your industry.
   - Allows you to showcase your professional skills and experience through your profile and share industry news and updates with your followers.
   - Offers advertising and recruiting solutions for businesses, making it a valuable tool for recruiting top talent and promoting products and services.

Disadvantages:
- It has a more formal tone and is not as suitable for sharing personal or casual content.
- It can be time consuming to build a strong presence on the platform and build valuable connections.
- Not as popular as other social media platforms, which may limit your reach to a wider audience.

Examples of successful LinkedIn pages: Microsoft, Forbes and Salesforce.

5. **YouTube** is a video sharing platform that allows users to upload and share videos with their audience. It is suitable for businesses and individuals who want to share educational, how-to or entertainment videos with their audience. The platform is also a valuable tool for content creators, bloggers and vloggers.

    Advantages:
    - It is a great platform for sharing video content including educational, how-to or entertainment videos.
    - Allows you to reach a wide audience, with over 2 billion active users worldwide.
    - Offers monetization options, such as advertising and sponsorships, for content creators.

    Disadvantages:
    - It can be time-consuming and require a significant investment in equipment and editing software to create high-quality video content.
    - It is primarily a visual platform, which may limit your reach to non-video audiences.
    - The algorithm can be unpredictable, which can affect your reach and visibility on the platform.

    Examples of successful YouTube channels: PewDiePie, Tasty and TED.

6. **TikTok** is a short-form video sharing platform that allows users to create and share 15-60 second videos with their audience. It is suitable for businesses and individuals who want to share fun, engaging and creative videos with a younger audience. The platform is also a valuable tool for influencers, content creators and brands.

    Advantages:
    - It's a great platform to reach a younger audience, with over 1 billion active users worldwide, most of whom are under 30 years old.
    - Allows you to create fun, engaging and creative videos using a variety of editing tools and effects.

- It offers a direct line of communication with your audience, making it a valuable tool for engaging and building a loyal following.

Disadvantages:

- The fast-paced nature of the platform can make it difficult to follow the latest trends and visibility.
- It takes a significant investment of time and creativity to create high-quality, engaging content that resonates with your audience.
- The algorithm can be unpredictable, which can affect your reach and visibility on the platform.

Examples of successful TikTok accounts: Charli D'Amelio, Addison Rae and The Washington Post.

7. **Reddit**: Reddit is a social news aggregator and discussion platform that allows users to share content and discuss various topics with other users in communities (called "subreddits"). It is suitable for businesses and individuals who want to engage in discussions and share content related to their industry or interests.

   Advantages:

   - It's a great platform to engage in discussions and share content related to your industry or interests.
   - Offers a huge range of communities (called "subreddits") covering various interests and topics, making it easy to find and connect with like-minded users.
   - It offers a direct line of communication with your audience, making it a valuable tool for engaging and building a loyal following.

   Disadvantages:

   - The platform has a steep learning curve and can be difficult to navigate for new users.
   - The anonymity of the platform can lead to trolls and negative comments that can affect your reputation.
   - It can be time consuming to build a strong presence on the platform and build valuable connections.

   Examples of successful subreddits: r/aww, r/science and r/personalfinance.

8. **Pinterest** is a social media platform that allows users to discover, save and share images and ideas related to their interests. It is suitable for businesses and individuals who want to present their products, services or ideas in a visually appealing way.

   Advantages:

• It's a great platform to drive traffic and sales to your website or online store, as users can click on the pins to be taken directly to the source.
• Allows you to showcase your products or services in a visually appealing way and provides opportunities to connect with potential customers.
• Offers a huge range of content categories and interests, making it easy to find and connect with like-minded users.

Disadvantages:
• It can be difficult to stand out among the millions of pins on the platform and gain visibility.
• The platform's algorithm may be unpredictable, which may affect your reach and visibility on the platform.
• Mainly used by women, which may not be ideal for businesses or individuals targeting a male audience.
Examples of successful Pinterest accounts: Etsy, Whole Foods Market, and HGTV.

9. **Snapchat** is a multimedia messaging app that allows users to share photos, videos and messages that disappear after a set period. It is suitable for businesses and individuals who want to connect with a younger, tech-savvy audience.

    Advantages:
    • It's a great platform to reach a younger audience, with over 90% of users under the age of 34.
    • Allows you to share fun, creative and engaging content using a variety of filters, stickers and lenses.
    • It offers a direct line of communication with your audience, making it a valuable tool for engaging and building a loyal following.

    Disadvantages:
    • The fast-paced nature of the platform can make it difficult to follow the latest trends and visibility.
    • Content disappears after a set period, which can make it difficult to build a strong presence and engagement with your audience.
    • It can be difficult to create high-quality content that resonates with your audience and fits the short time frame.
    Examples of successful Snapchat accounts: Kylie Jenner, NBA and McDonald's.

10. **Clubhouse** is an audio-only social networking app that allows users to engage in real-time, voice-based conversations with others on a variety of topics. It is

suitable for businesses and individuals who want to join discussions and share their expertise on a specific topic.

Advantages:

• It is a great platform to join discussions and share your experience on a particular topic.

• Offers a direct line of communication with your audience and others, making it a valuable tool for engaging and making valuable connections.

• It is a unique platform that offers a fresh and innovative approach to social media.

Disadvantages:

• Currently only available for iOS users, limiting the potential audience and reach.

• The fast-paced nature of the platform can make it difficult to keep track of the latest conversations and view.

• A significant investment of time is required to engage in valuable conversations and build a strong presence on the platform.

There are and will be more and more media similar to the above. Start with the most well-known since getting started with any of them takes time and patience. I hope this kind of research that I do for you will be useful for you. It's a good idea to google for example what social media exists to see how many others are out there.

****

I'm giving you a few things that will help you get more of an audience in whatever you do, in order to help you as much as I can with this book and save you a lot of time in searching. Not everyone may be interested in everything in this book. But I wanted it to be a book with practical solutions and examples and not just general theories. You can find more at my blog.

****

Here are some strategies that can help drive more people to your website and YouTube channel:

1. Make sure your website and YouTube channel are **well organized and easy to navigate**. Use relevant keywords in your titles, descriptions and tags, and create eye-catching visuals that reflect your brand.

2. **Create content that is valuable**, informative and entertaining for your target audience. This can include blog posts, videos, infographics, podcasts, and other

types of content that showcase your expertise and provide value to your audience.

3. **Use Social Media**: Share your content on social media channels to reach a wider audience. Use hashtags, tags and mentions to increase your visibility and attract new followers.

4. **Engage with your audience by responding to comments**, hosting Q&A sessions, and asking for feedback. And asking them to tell you their opinion (feedback) and asking for their advice. This helps build a community around your brand and encourages people to keep coming back.

5. **Offer incentives**, such as exclusive content or discounts, to encourage people to visit your website or YouTube channel. This can help build your email list or grow your subscriber base.

6. **Partner with other creators** or brands in your industry or niche to reach new audiences and expand your network. This can include guest appearances, co-hosting webinars or collaborating on projects.

7. **Paid advertising** can be a quick and effective way to reach new audiences. Consider using social media ads or Google AdWords to target your ideal audience with your content and promotions.

8. Make sure your website and YouTube channel **are optimized for search engines** so that people can easily find you when they search for relevant keywords or phrases. Use tools like Google Analytics to monitor your search engine rankings and traffic.

9. **Offer something super cool for free**: Offer something free, like free trials or samples, to encourage people to try your products or services. This can help build trust and loyalty among your target audience.

10. **Host events**, such as webinars or live streams, to engage with and provide value to your audience. This can help you establish yourself as an authority in your niche and attract more followers.

11. **Partner with influencers** in your industry or niche to promote your content and reach new audiences. Influencers can help amplify your message and build credibility among their followers.

12. **Run contests and giveaways** to encourage people to interact with your brand and promote your content. This can help you increase your reach and attract more followers to your website and YouTube channel.

13. **Create shareable content**: Create content that people will want to share with others. This can be anything from an instructional video to a fun meme. By

creating shareable content, you can reach new audiences and increase your visibility online.

14. **Use email marketing** to keep your subscribers updated on your latest content and offers. This can be an effective way to increase traffic to your website and YouTube channel as well as build relationships with your audience.

15. **Leverage Social Media Groups**: Join and participate in relevant social media groups to connect with like-minded people and promote your content. Just make sure you follow the group rules and participate in a way that provides value to the community.

16. Remember that it is important to **focus on quality** and not just quantity when it comes to building an audience. Providing valuable content.

17. **Using Search Engine Optimization (SEO):** Use SEO techniques to promote your website and YouTube channel for search engines. This can help improve your rankings and make it easier for people to find your content online.

18. **Offer something free that they'll learn something useful for them**: Offer an ebook or whitepaper in exchange for signing up for your email list or following you on social media. This can help you build your email list and grow your social media following and provide value to your audience.

19. **Create attractive thumbnails and titles** for your YouTube videos to attract attention and increase your views. The same goes for your featured images and website headlines - they should be visually appealing and attention-grabbing.

****

Passive income is income you earn without having to actively work for it on a regular basis. **Here are some ways to generate passive income:**

1. **Rental income** is generated by renting out property that you own, such as a house, apartment or commercial space. The amount of rental income you can generate depends on the location of the property, the condition of the property and rental rates in the area. Rental income can be a great source of passive income, but it does require some initial investment and ongoing management, such as finding tenants, collecting rent, and maintaining the property.

2. **Dividend income** is generated by owning dividend paying stocks. Dividends are a portion of a company's earnings paid out to shareholders. The amount of dividend income you can generate depends on the size of your investment and the dividend yield of the stocks you own. Dividend income is generally seen as a more stable and reliable source of passive income compared to other forms of investment, but it does require some initial investment and ongoing

management, such as monitoring the performance of your stocks. Choose stocks from companies that are big names (giants) and you love their products.

3. **Interest income** is generated by investing in fixed income securities such as bonds, certificates of deposits (CDs) or savings accounts. The amount of interest income you can generate depends on the interest rate on the security and the amount of money you invest. Interest income is generally considered a low-risk and reliable source of passive income, but it does require some initial investment and ongoing management, such as monitoring interest rates and managing your investments.

4. **Royalties** are payments made to the owner of an intellectual property, such as a book, song or invention, for the use or sale of that property. The amount of royalties you can generate depends on the popularity and demand for your intellectual property. Royalties can be a great source of passive income if you've created popular intellectual property, but it requires some initial investment in creating the intellectual property and ongoing management, such as tracking the use and sale of your property.

5. **Affiliate marketing** (no need to invest money in this): Affiliate marketing involves promoting products or services on your website or social media channels and earning a commission on any resulting sales (**you sell other people's stuff at a percentage from each sale**). The amount of passive income you can generate from affiliate marketing depends on the number of sales you generate and the commission rate your affiliate program offers. Many places offer you ready-made promotion tools such as texts, posters, videos, etc. You take them and use them on your page and in your social media. Affiliate marketing can be a great source of passive income if you have a large following or highly engaged audience, but it requires ongoing management, such as choosing the right products to promote and tracking your affiliate links.

6. **Digital Products**: Digital products are products created and sold online, such as e-books, online courses or software. The amount of passive income you can generate from digital products depends on the popularity and demand for those products. Digital products can be a great source of passive income if you have a unique or in-demand product or sell others with a percentage of each sale, but it requires an initial investment in creating the product and ongoing management such as marketing and customer support or if they are others, no investment is needed.

7. **Peer-to-peer lending platforms** allow you to lend money to individuals or businesses and earn interest on the loans. Especially in poor countries where a small amount from you can be huge for them. The amount of passive income you can generate from peer-to-peer lending depends on the interest rate on the loans and the amount of money you lend. Peer-to-peer lending can be a

great source of passive income if you have extra cash to invest, but it does require some initial investment and ongoing management, such as choosing the right loans to invest in and monitoring your loan performance.

8. **Overall**, creating passive income requires some initial investment (for most) and ongoing management, but it can be a great way to build a long-term, reliable source of income. It is important to research and understand the various options available and choose the ones that align with your goals, interests and abilities.

9. **Build a Mobile App**: Building a successful mobile app can provide a passive income stream through in-app purchases or ad revenue.

10. **Investing in real estate crowdfunding**: Real estate crowdfunding platforms allow investors to pool their money to invest in real estate projects, providing a passive income through rental income or profit sharing.

11. **Create and sell an online course**: Creating an online course in a field you are knowledgeable in can provide a passive income stream through sales.

12. Create a YouTube Channel: Creating a popular YouTube channel can provide a passive income stream through advertising revenue.

13. **Dividend index funds and exchange traded funds.**

14. **Bonds and bond index funds.**

15. **High yield savings accounts.**

16. **Sell the photos you take**. There are places where you put the photos you take and companies and advertisers go there looking for specific photos to promote products and services.

17. In some **online games** you can make useful products that will be bought by users.

There are other ways but I don't know how much you will be interested in this topic and I don't want to bore you. Type in google the best ways for passive income, to get other suggestions.

****

Finding one's purpose in life is a deeply personal and often ongoing journey. **Here are some steps that may help one discover their purpose**:

1. **Think about your passions and interests:** Think about the things you enjoy doing or are curious to try. What subjects or activities are you drawn to? These can give you clues about your natural inclinations and passions.

2. **Don't be bored, take a pen and paper and write them down! How else will you be able to remember everything you thought and analyze it afterwards?**

3. **Think about what makes you feel fulfilled**: Think about the times when you feel most fulfilled or happy. What activities or experiences are you engaged in at these moments that make you feel so full and covered and excited and awestruck? These may be times when you felt proud of an accomplishment, experienced a sense of purpose, or felt a deep connection with others. What were those experiences that made you feel fulfilled? This can help you identify the values and activities that are most important to you.

4. **Think about your values**: Think about your core values and beliefs. What matters most to you? What are the principles that guide your life? Do you value creativity, honesty, kindness, social justice, or some other principle? How can you live a life that is aligned with these values?

5. **Try new experiences**: Sometimes, we may not know what we are interested in until we try something new. Consider trying new experiences, hobbies or careers to see what resonates with you. Consider taking a class, attending a workshop, or volunteering for a cause you care about. This can help you broaden your horizons and gain new ideas. Because everything new you learn is not lost. You can do it step by step tutorials. Or YouTube videos and get an audience and maybe a passive income from it!

6. **Seek guidance from others**: Talking with friends, family members, or a therapist can help you gain insight and clarity about your purpose. You may have a "gift" that you do not know you have because for you it is just an easy habit. So, you don't see it as your calling and a third party who sees it can guide you to realize it!

7. **Consider your passions and interests**: Consider your hobbies, interests, and activities that make you lose track of time. Think about the types of books, movies, or TV shows you like. Do you have any particular areas of expertise or knowledge that interest you? What would you do if you had unlimited time and resources? All of these are possible clues to your passions and interests.

8. **Identify your strengths**: Think about the skills and talents that come naturally to you. Think about the things you excel at that come easily to you. You can also ask friends, family members or colleagues for their input on your strengths. This can help you identify areas where you can excel and make a meaningful contribution. Think about the things you are good at or have been complimented on.

9. **Keep an open mind**: Remember that discovering your purpose is a process and may not happen overnight. Be open to new experiences, be curious and be willing to explore different paths and opportunities. Remember that your

purpose can evolve over time, so be open to adaptation and change as you continue to grow and learn.

****

If you're looking to identify your strengths and find out what you're good at, here are some tips that might help:

1. **Take a self-assessment test**: There are several free online tools that can help you identify your strengths and weaknesses (such as the CliftonStrengths assessment or the VIA Character Strengths survey.). These tests can help you determine what you're good at and what you might need to improve on. For a quick look at your personal and professional strengths (and weaknesses), check out some of these short tests and worksheets work.
Personal SWOT analysis.
Leadership Legacy Assessment.
Situational Strengths Test (SST)
Strength Regulation Worksheet.
My Strengths and Qualities Worksheet.
The HIGH5 Strengths Test.
Look it up on google. In the links and suggestions, I write to you that concern specific media, by the time you read this book, some will not exist, others will not be free anymore and other news will have come out.
2. **Ask friends**, relatives, colleagues. We analyzed it above.
3. **Try new things**. We analyzed it above.
4. **Think about your successes**: Think about the times when you have achieved something that you are proud of. What skills did you use to achieve this success? This can help you identify your strengths and areas in which you excel.
5. **Use your values as a guide**: Consider your core values and what is important to you. If you are passionate about a particular cause or activity, it can be an indication of your strengths.
6. **Think about what you do naturally** - innately - very easily: Think about the things you find easy or effortless to do. You may not have thought about them before, but they could be a strong indicator of your natural abilities.
7. **Analyze your achievements**: Look back at your achievements and think about what skills and abilities you used to achieve them. This can help you identify your areas of strength.
8. **Take note of compliments**: Pay attention to the compliments you receive from others. What do people praise you for? This can help you determine what you are good at.

9. Don't be afraid to **try new things** and explore your interests. You might discover new talents and passions you didn't know you had (hopefully positive and not negative haha).

10. **Look for patterns**: Pay attention to the patterns in your life. What types of activities or tasks consistently bring you joy and satisfaction? This can be an indication of your strengths.

11. **Keep a journal**: Recording your thoughts and reflections can help you spot patterns and ideas about your strengths and interests.

12. **Take classes or workshops**: Consider taking classes or workshops on a variety of subjects to see what interests you and where you excel.

13. Remember, identifying your strengths is only the first step. It is important to develop and use these strengths to achieve your goals and live a fulfilling life. So, once you've identified your strengths, find ways to apply them to your personal and professional life.

****

If someone is constantly thinking that they don't have money, it can be difficult to shift their mindset to a more positive one but there are ways they can do it if they want to. Here are some tips that can help:

1. **Practice Gratitude**: Instead of focusing on what you don't have, try focusing on what you do have. Make a list of things you are grateful for. Take some time each day to reflect on the things you are grateful for, no matter how small they may seem. This can help you cultivate a sense of abundance and contentment.

2. **Reframe your thoughts**: When you catch yourself having negative thoughts about money, try to reframe those thoughts in a more positive way. For example, instead of thinking "I don't have enough money," try thinking "**I have enough to meet my basic needs and I'm working to improve my financial situation.**"

3. **Surround yourself with positive influences**: Try to surround yourself with people who are positive and supportive and who can help you stay focused on your goals. **STOP** talking about the fact that you do not have money to pay your obligations, for vacations, etc.

4. **Take Action**: Instead of worrying about your financial situation, focus on taking steps to improve it. This may mean looking for ways to make more money or finding ways to save money and cut expenses. Take action on creating a passive income.

5. **Practice self-care**: Take care of yourself physically, mentally and emotionally. Get enough sleep, exercise regularly and make time for relaxation and hobbies.

6. **Focus on the present**: Instead of worrying about the future, focus on the present moment and what you can do now to improve your situation.
7. **Believe in yourself**: Believe that you have the ability to create a life of abundance and prosperity and that you are capable of achieving your goals. Develop a growth mindset and be open to learning and trying new things.
8. **Visualize Success**: Take some time each day to imagine yourself financially secure and achieving your goals. This can help you stay motivated and positive. **Spend some time each day visualizing the abundance you want to create in your life. Imagine yourself living in a comfortable home, driving a nice car and enjoying financial freedom.** This can help you shift your focus from lack to abundance and attract more positive outcomes.
9. **Focus on what you can control**: While it's important to recognize your financial situation and take steps to improve it, it's just as important to focus on what you can control. Make a plan to save money, reduce your expenses and increase your income. Focus on taking small, achievable steps that will move you in the right direction.
10. **Do all the steps from this book! All of them! You have so many tools in this book use them!**

****

Here are some things one can do every day to help them grow, think positively and feel joy: Let's sum them up.

1. Gratitude.
2. Practice being present in the moment.
3. Exercise. Regular exercise can help improve your mood and reduce stress.
4. Learning: Take time to learn something new every day, whether it's a new skill or just reading a book. This can help stimulate your mind and give you a sense of accomplishment. And it helps you not to constantly think about what you don't have and to be filled you with enthusiasm. There are so many videos, tutorials and free seminars with different things to learn and all for free! Look it up on google and YouTube.
5. Talk to the ones you love: Spend time with loved ones, either in person or virtually (viper, zoom, skype, etc.). Having positive relationships can help boost your mood and make you feel more connected to others.
6. Self-care. Enjoy your bath, listening to your music, etc.
7. Set goals: Set small (beyond your long-range goals), achievable goals for yourself and focus by taking action towards them every day. This can give you a sense of purpose and help you feel more productive.

8. Laughter: Find something to laugh about every day, whether it's a funny video or a conversation with a friend. Laughter can boost your mood and make you feel happier.
9. Remember, things that work for one person may not work for another person. It's important to find what works for you and make it a regular part of your daily routine.
10. Volunteering: Give to your community or somewhere that is needed: your time, money, your knowledge, a good conversation. This can give you a sense of purpose and help you feel more connected to others.
11. Find time to do something you love: Take time every day to do something you really enjoy, whether it's reading, painting, or just spending time with your pet or at an animal shelter. This can help you feel more fulfilled and happier in your daily life.

****

As you can see some steps such as gratitude is a basic and necessary step in many topics that is why I write them again and again. And not because I want to bore you or to fill pages. ************************

When someone thinks all day long about how bad they are in this or that…..Here are some tips on how they can try reverse that:

1. Start by **identifying any negative self-talk** you engage in, then challenge those negative thoughts. For example, if you catch yourself thinking, "I'm not good enough," challenge that thought by asking yourself: " **Why I am not good enough? Is there evidence to support this belief?**" You may realize that there is no real evidence to support this belief and that it is just a thought that has become a habit. Or if you say "yeah then…" reexamine the situation did something else even better happen because you didn't do it right back then? Or maybe it was not your fault that the circumstances were like they were?
2. **Focus on your strengths**: Instead of dwelling on your weaknesses, focus on your strengths. Write them down. Identify your unique talents and skills and find ways to use them to your advantage. For example, if you are good at writing, start a blog or write articles for a website. As long as you do this by emphasizing your good points, you **won't focus on what you don't know**.
3. **Practice self-compassion**: Treat yourself with kindness and compassion as you would a friend in trouble. Recognize that everyone has strengths and weaknesses and that it's okay to make mistakes.
4. **Set realistic goals**: Set achievable goals that align with your strengths and values. Even with your daily should and wants. Start with small, manageable goals that you can build towards over time. This will help you build confidence and self-

esteem. Did you manage to do as much as you wanted today? Celebrate it like a victory! You found the time to enjoy a ride is a victory celebrate it!

5. **Take action**!
6. If someone constantly thinks that they are not good enough at their job, they can try **to identify why they feel that way**. Perhaps they have received criticism in the past or are compared to their colleagues. Once they **identify the source of their negative thoughts**, they can challenge those thoughts by focusing on their strengths and accomplishments. They can also practice self-compassion by recognizing that everyone makes mistakes and that it's okay to ask for help when they need it. Try this on everything you say you're not good at.
7. Try the technique that **erases beliefs** that is been given to you in one of the upper pages of this book (page 41-42).
8. Sometimes the best way to combat negative thoughts is to take action. Make a plan to **improve in areas where you feel insecure or lacking** and take steps towards your goals. For example, if you feel like you're not a strong writer, take a writing class or join a writing group to improve your skills.
9. **Reframe negative self-talk**: Once you challenge your negative self-talk, try to reframe it in a more positive and constructive way. This can help you see the situation from a different perspective and feel more positive.
Example: "Although I may not have all the skills required for this job, I can learn and improve over time. I will focus on my strengths and work hard to develop new skills."
10. **Challenge the "should" and "must"**: Negative self-talk often includes "should for actions/responsibilities/duties that were making us happy or we believed we needed them. And "must" is used for actions/responsibilities/tasks that are considered mandatory/necessary. That are unrealistic or unhelpful now or at the beginning. Challenge these thoughts by asking yourself if they are reasonable and helpful now. Once it may have been but do, they still are? Stop those must to do things (activities) if they are not making you happy anymore.
11. **Make your weaknesses a passive income.** Write about them! For example: Five ways to fail at........ Show others how not to do it so they can learn what to avoid!

****

Here are some details and examples of small changes that can help someone learn to love themselves.

1. Try the techniques I suggested at 41-42 page of the book (touching your body in 2 different ways).
2. Pay attention to the language you use when you talk to yourself. If you find yourself being overly judgmental, try reframing your thoughts in a more positive way.

For example, instead of saying "I'm so stupid," try saying "**I made a mistake, but I'll learn from it and do better next time.**"
Instead of saying, "I can't do that," try saying "**I may struggle with this, but I'll keep trying and ask for help if I need it.**"
Instead of saying, "I hate my body," try saying "**My body is unique and special and I am grateful for everything it does for me.**"
Instead of saying "I'm a failure," try saying: "**I faced a setback but I will not give up. I will continue to work hard and strive for the best**".
Instead of saying "I'm not good enough," try saying: "**I am worthy and capable and will continue to push myself to achieve my goals**"
Instead of saying "I'm so unlucky," try saying: "**Things didn't go my way this time, but I'll keep a positive attitude and look for opportunities in the future.**"

3. Set healthy boundaries: It is important to prioritize your own needs and set boundaries with others. This means saying no when you need to and not feeling guilty about it. For example, if a friend wants you to hang out but you're feeling exhausted, it's okay to decline and prioritize your rest.

4. Take care of your body: Loving yourself also means taking care of your physical health. This includes getting enough sleep, eating nutritious foods, and doing physical activity that you enjoy.

5. Take time to do things that make you feel good, whether it's reading a book, taking a bubble bath, or listening to your favorite music, etc. Make self-care a regular part of your routine.

6. Spend time with people who lift your spirits, cheer you up and support you. It can be friends, family or even online communities. Make a conscious effort to cut negative influences out of your life.

7. Take time each day to reflect on the things in your life that you are grateful for. This can help you shift your thoughts from negative to positive.

8. Forgive yourself: We all make mistakes and have moments of weakness. It is important to practice self-forgiveness and let go of past mistakes. Treat yourself with the same kindness and understanding you would extend to a friend.

9. Positive Affirmations: Self-love includes the ability to see yourself in a positive light. One way to cultivate positive self-talk is through daily positive affirmations. These are statements that you can repeat to yourself to reinforce positive beliefs in yourself. For example, "I am capable and worthy of love and success" or "I love and accept myself just the way I am" etc.

10. Gratitude Journal: Record the small beautiful events of the day. It can be small things like a warm cup of tea you drank and felt calm or a good conversation with a friend. Anything that brought you peace and joy. You record it to focus on the positive and beautiful things of your day.

11. Mindfulness meditation involves sitting quietly and observing your thoughts without judgment. This helps develop present moment awareness and can lead to increased self-acceptance and self-love. Take time each day to practice mindfulness meditation, even if it's just for a few minutes.

12. Self-reflection: Take time to explore your thoughts, feelings, and beliefs. You can do this by journaling, meditating, or simply spending time alone with your thoughts. Think about your beliefs and try to identify any negative beliefs that may be holding you back.

13. Pay attention to situations or people that cause negative thoughts or negative feelings. By understanding what triggers these negative beliefs, thoughts, and feelings you can begin to recognize and challenge them.

14. Surround yourself with positive influences: The people, what you read or see and media you surround yourself with can have a significant impact on your beliefs and self-talk. Look for positive influences such as books, podcasts or people who lift you up and inspire you. Limit exposure to negative influences such as news or social media that trigger negative thoughts and feelings.

15. Get help: Consider working with a therapist or counselor who can help you identify and challenge negative beliefs. A professional can help you gain a deeper understanding of your beliefs and offer strategies to change them.

16. For example, let's say you have a deep-seated belief that you're not good enough to succeed in your career. You can reflect on why you have this belief and challenge it by reminding yourself of moments of success. You could also look for positive affirmations or mantras to repeat to yourself, such as "**I am capable and worthy of success.**" Additionally, you might seek out a mentor or expert who can provide guidance and support as you work to change your beliefs. Negative beliefs often appear as automatic thoughts that you don't even realize you're having. If you become aware of these thoughts, you can begin to challenge them. Once you identify a negative belief, challenge it by asking yourself questions like, "Is this belief true?" or "Where did this belief come from?" Sometimes negative beliefs are based on false assumptions or past experiences that are no longer relevant. Replace negative beliefs with positive ones: Instead of just trying to get rid of negative beliefs, it's important to replace them with positive ones. And finally, don't forget that I have also suggested a technique (page 41-42) that I personally tried and was surprised by the results.

17. Sometimes, it can be difficult to recognize our own negative beliefs and thought patterns. Consider seeking feedback from people you trust, such as friends, family or a therapist. Ask them to help you identify negative self-talk or limiting beliefs that may be holding you back.

18. Use cognitive-behavioral therapy (CBT) techniques: CBT is a type of therapy that can help you identify and challenge negative beliefs and patterns in your

thinking. A CBT therapist can teach you techniques to reframe negative thoughts, challenge negative beliefs, and develop positive coping strategies.

19. The application of philosophy to everyday problems. Find yourself doing philosophical counseling. It does not cost much.

****

It can be difficult to find ways to benefit from a difficult situation, but it is not impossible. Here are some suggestions that may help:

1. **Use it as motivation**: Difficult times can be great motivation to make positive changes in your life. Use the experience to push yourself to work harder. To be more focused and strive for more important goals. When you overcome a difficult situation, it can be incredibly empowering and motivating.
2. **Help others**: Use the hardship you went through to help others who may be going through a similar experience. Share your story through video and a blog or by providing any support to others. You can help others meet challenges and come out stronger. This can also give you a sense of purpose and meaning.
3. Going through tough times can **help you build resilience**, which is a valuable skill in all areas of life. The ability to bounce back from adversity can help you handle future challenges with greater ease and confidence.
4. Sometimes the best way to take advantage of a difficult time is to **turn it into a creative outlet**. Use the experience to create art, write a book or start a blog or in video form to publish. By sharing your story through a creative medium, you can help others while benefiting yourself.
5. Remember that taking advantage of a difficult time it's about **finding value** and growth in difficult situations.
6. Difficult times often require **resilience**, which is the ability to bounce back and recover from setbacks. Resilience is like a muscle that can be strengthened through practice. One way to practice resilience is to challenge negative thoughts and replace them with more positive and empowering ones.
7. **Learn from experience**: Difficult times can be an opportunity for learning and growth. It can be helpful to reflect on the experience and ask yourself what you can learn from it. Maybe you discovered a new strength or weakness. Or that you gained new ideas and perspectives.
8. Going through difficult times can create **empathy** and understanding for others going through similar challenges. This can create an opportunity to connect with others and be offered support and encouragement, or to offer it yourself.
9. A difficult time can also provide an opportunity to **discover new passions** and interests. Sometimes when we are forced out of our comfort zone, we can find joy and fulfillment in unexpected places.

10. **Re-evaluate priorities**: In difficult times, it can be helpful to re-evaluate priorities and focus on what is most important in life. This can create an opportunity to align values and goals with actions and make positive changes.
11. Pour it into **gratitude**.
12. **Seek support**: It is important to seek support during difficult times, whether from friends, family or a professional. This can provide an opportunity to connect with others and receive guidance and encouragement to suffer less.
13. For example, if someone is going through a difficult time, such as losing a job, they may feel overwhelmed and hopeless. However, by practicing resilience and positive thinking, they may see job loss as an opportunity to reassess their career goals and discover new interests and new abilities they didn't know they had. They may also turn to their network for support and guidance, which could lead to new job opportunities or personal growth. And why not change careers to something better.

****

Here are more details and examples of each of the tools that can be helpful in setting goals, overcoming obstacles, generating website traffic, getting in shape, and toward personal happiness:

1. **Tools for your goals:** Some popular goal setting tools include keeping a journal. Creating a collage board with as many photos as you want and maybe using a goal setting app. Journaling includes recording your goals and tracking your progress, which can help you stay accountable and motivated. A collage board is a visual representation of your goals and dreams that can serve as a daily reminder of what you're aiming for. Goal setting apps like Todoist or Trello can help you break down your goals into manageable tasks and track your progress. There are programs for mobile to make your plan and your lists with what you have to do (a planner or a to-do list app).

Example: Let's say your goal is to run a marathon. You could create a collage board of images of runners crossing the finish line, set a goal in a goal-setting app. Run a certain number of miles each week and track your progress in a journal.

Example: If someone wants to start a business, they can use a program to write their plan and schedule their tasks and deadlines. A collage board to visualize his success and a to-do list app to track his progress.

2. **Tools for overcoming obstacles:** Some tools that can help you overcome obstacles include positive self-talk, meditation, and therapy. Positive self-talk involves consciously replacing negative thoughts with positive ones, which can help change your mindset and build resilience. Meditation can help you manage

stress and anxiety, which can be major obstacles to achieving your goals. Therapy can help you address deeper issues that may be holding you back.

Example: Let's say you have a fear of public speaking and it's holding you back from advancing in your career. You could practice positive self-talk by telling yourself that you are capable and confident. You could also try meditating before a big presentation to calm your nerves. You could try the technique for erasing beliefs that I have suggested. If your fear of public speaking is rooted in deeper issues, therapy could help you work through those issues and build confidence.

3. **Website traffic generation tools**: Some tools that can help you generate traffic to your web pages include search engine optimization (SEO), social media marketing, and email marketing. SEO involves optimizing your website so that it ranks higher in search engine results, which can lead to more traffic to your website. Social media marketing involves promoting your website on social media platforms, which can help you reach a wider audience. Email marketing involves sending regular newsletters or updates to your subscribers, which can help build relationships and increase traffic to your website.

Example: Let's say you're a small business owner with a website that sells handmade jewelry. You could use SEO techniques to optimize your site for keywords like "handmade jewelry" or "unique accessories." You could also use social media platforms like Instagram or Facebook to showcase your products and drive traffic to your website. Finally, you could send regular newsletters to your subscribers with updates on new products or sales as well as useful jewelry cleaning and maintenance tips.

4. **Fitness tools**: Some tools that can help you get fit include fitness apps, wearable fitness trackers, and online workout videos. Fitness apps like Nike Training Club or MyFitnessPal can help you track your progress and have customized workout plans. Wearable fitness trackers like the Fitbit or Apple Watch can track your activity and provide real-time feedback. Online workout videos like those found on YouTube can provide free workouts you can do at home.

Example: Let's say you want to start running to get in shape. You could download an app like C25K or MapMyRun to track your progress and have customized training plans. You could also use a watch or an app on your phone that tells you your heart rate and calories and steps taken and burned to track your activity and track your progress. Finally, you could find free running workouts on YouTube to help you get started.

5. **Tools to feel happier**: Some tools that can help you be happier include gratitude journals, mindfulness practices, and self-care activities. Mindfulness practices like meditation or yoga can help you be more present and reduce stress.

****

Here are some details and examples of how someone who hates their job can make small daily changes to stop feeling that way:

1. **Take breaks**: Taking breaks during the day can help break the monotony and give you a chance to recharge. Go for a short walk, read a book or listen to music.
2. **Find something to look forward to**: Plan something outside of work that you will look forward to do. It could be as simple as meeting a friend for lunch or as complex as planning a vacation.
3. **Learn something new**: Try to learn something new, even if it's something small. This could be as simple as learning a new word each day, trying a new recipe or taking an online course.
4. **Focus on the positive**: Instead of focusing on the negative aspects of your job, try to focus on the positive. This can be anything from enjoying the company of your colleagues to the feeling of accomplishment when you complete a task. And that from your salary you pay everything that you need to.
5. **Connect with others**: Connecting with others can help you feel less alone and isolated at work. This could be as simple as starting a conversation with a colleague or joining a professional group.
6. **Start a gratitude journal**: Each day, write down three things you are grateful for. This can help shift your focus away from the negative and towards the positive.
7. **Explore new job opportunities**: If you are really unhappy in your job, consider exploring new job opportunities. Get started by updating your resume and networking with others in your field even online and in groups.
8. Start working on **having passive income** so that at some point you will not need this job.
9. **Change your mindset**: Start your day with a positive attitude and remind yourself of the things you are grateful for. This can help you shift your focus from what you don't like about your job to things in your life that bring you joy and fulfillment. Example: Before you get out of bed, take a few minutes to visualize something positive that you will look forward to throughout the day, such as having lunch with a friend, going for a walk outside, or watching your favorite show.
10. **Make small changes to your routine**: Change something small in your daily routine that will help you feel better. It could be something as simple as taking a different route to work or listening to an engaging podcast on your way to and from work.
    Example: If you usually drive to work, try taking public transportation one day a week. Use the time on the bus or train to start a book you've been wanting to read or to meditate and center yourself before starting your day. Or to see funny videos.

11. **Connect with your colleagues**: Building positive relationships with your colleagues can make a huge difference in how you feel about your work. Try to get to know your colleagues and find ways to support each other.
Example: Start a group where you go for a walk with your colleagues, where you can get some exercise, fresh air and social interaction all at the same time.

12. **Find ways to bring your passions to work**: Look for opportunities to incorporate your passions and interests into your work, even if they don't seem directly connected.
Example: If you enjoy writing, see if you can take on some extra copywriting projects or offer to proofread your colleagues' work. If you enjoy organizing events, volunteer to organize someone's office birthday party.

13. **Start planning your next career move**: If you really hate your job and see no way to improve it, start thinking about what you'd like to do. Take some time to explore your options and create a plan to make a career change.
Example: Start by researching careers that align with your interests and strengths. You could also take a class or workshop to develop new skills, or consider going back to school to get a degree in a different field.

****

There are several changes one can make in their daily life to have more time to enjoy life and be happier and more positive. Here are some examples:

1. **Priority**: Prioritize having time for you too. Focus on what really matters to you. Determine what the most important tasks/to-dos are and do them first.

2. **Eliminate the activities that make you waste your time**: Identify (See What They Are) the activities that waste time and eliminate them. This can include things like hanging out on social media, watching too much TV shows- movies (Cut the long hours on TV and social media), or engaging in activities that no longer bring you joy or value.

3. **Practice Mindfulness**: Take a few minutes each day to practice Mindfulness. This can be as simple as focusing on your breathing, paying attention to your surroundings, or taking a moment to appreciate the little things in life.

4. **Exercise – work out**.

5. **Spend time with your loved ones**.

6. **Start having a hobby**. It's a great way to reduce stress and increase your happiness. Whether playing an instrument, painting, cooking or whatever, **find something that brings you joy and make time for it**.

7. **Get enough sleep**.

8. **Simplify your schedule**: Reduce the number of commitments in your schedule to spend more time on things you enjoy. This may mean cutting

back on work hours or social obligations. Or the activities that no longer fill you but you do them out of habit.

9. **Spend time in nature**: Spending time in nature has been shown to reduce stress and improve mood. Even a short walk in a park or a few minutes sitting outside can make a big difference.
10. **Take breaks**: Take regular breaks throughout the day to recharge and avoid burnout. This might mean going for a walk, reading a book, or simply taking a few deep breaths or see a funny video.
11. **Embrace change and try new things**. This can help you break out of old habits and routines and increase feelings of excitement and fulfillment in your life.
12. Remember, **small changes in your daily life** can have a big impact on your overall happiness and well-being. It's important to prioritize self-care and make time for the things that matter most to you. As we grow older, our needs also change, so what doesn't fill you, change it, don't continue it. You used to get fill of this activity now you don't. Replace it with something that fills you up.

****

Here are some things one can do to improve their mood, even when they feel angry:

1. **Acknowledge your feelings**: Find how you feel and accept your feelings, this is the first step to feeling better. It's okay to be angry, sad, or frustrated, but it's important to accept these feelings and not try to suppress them. Try to identify the root cause of your anger and deal with it accordingly. Note the situations, people or events that trigger your anger. Once you understand what triggers you, you can take steps to avoid or manage those triggers.
Example: If you get angry when someone interrupts you while you're talking, you can try politely asking them to let you finish speaking before answering.
2. Follow the techniques written "page 41-42" of the book.
3. **Take deep breaths**: Deep breathing can help reduce stress and calm the mind. Inhale slowly through your nose, hold for a few seconds, and exhale slowly through your mouth. Repeat this several times until you feel more relaxed.
4. **Engage in something that involves physical activity**: Tire yourself out. Exercise is a natural mood booster. Even a short walk outside can help improve your mood. Physical activity releases endorphins, which are chemicals that help reduce stress and anxiety. Regular exercise will help you not get angry as often.
5. **Listen to music**: Music can be a powerful mood booster. Choose music that you like and that makes you feel good. You can also create a playlist of your favorite songs that can cheer you up whenever you need it.

6. **Talk to others**: Social connection is important for mental health. Reach out to a friend or family member and talk to them about how you're feeling. You can also join a support group or join an online community and chat there to forget.
7. **Do something that makes you happy**: Engage in an activity you enjoy, whether it's reading a book, cooking or watching a movie. Doing something that makes you happy can distract you from negative thoughts and boost your mood.
8. **Start thinking about everything you are grateful for.**
9. **Go and do one of your hobbies**
10. **Go and have a relaxing bath or a massage.**
11. **Challenging negative thoughts**: When you catch yourself having negative thoughts, challenge them. Ask yourself if there is evidence to support these thoughts or if there is another, more positive way of looking at the situation.
12. **Laugh**: Laughter is a great way to improve your mood. Watch a funny movie, read a humorous book or watch funny videos or spend time with someone who makes you laugh.
13. **Use positive self-talk**: Replace negative thoughts and self-talk with positive affirmations. Tell yourself that you can handle the situation and that you are able to control your anger.
Example: "**I am in control of my emotions. I can stay calm and handle this situation.**"
14. **Take a time out**: When you feel your anger escalating, take a break from the situation. Go for a walk, take a few minutes to breathe, or do something else to calm yourself down.
Example: If you're in an argument with someone, say "**I need to take a break for a few minutes to calm down. Let's talk about it later.**"
15. **Communicate assertively**: Instead of lashing out in anger, express your feelings and needs in a clear, assertive way.
Example: " **I feel upset when** you interrupt me **while** I'm talking. **I would appreciate it if you** let me finish before you reply."
16. **Seek support**: If you are having trouble managing your anger on your own, seek support from a therapist, from a support group, or a trusted friend or family member.
Example: "I've been having trouble controlling my anger lately and I'd like to talk to a therapist to learn some strategies to manage it»
17. **Practice forgiveness**: Holding grudges and waiting for revenge can fuel anger and resentment over time. Practicing forgiveness, both of yourself and others, can help you let go of these negative feelings.
Example: Instead of focusing on the wrongs someone has done to you, try to focus on their positive qualities and the things you appreciate about them.
18. **Use humor**: Humor can be a powerful tool for relieving tension and anger.

Example: If you find yourself getting angry during a tense situation, try to find something funny or light about the situation to laugh at.

****

Emotional eating, or eating for reasons other than physical hunger, can be a common behavior for people when they feel bored, stressed, or lonely. However, this behavior can lead to unhealthy eating habits, weight gain and negative feelings about oneself. **Here are some suggestions on how to stop eating when you're bored or lonely:**

1. **Start by identifying what triggers your emotional eating**. Keep a diary and write down what you eat, when you eat and how you feel before and after eating. This can help you recognize patterns in your behavior and feelings. Note which situations or feelings trigger your emotional eating. Is it boring? Stress? Loneliness? Once you know your triggers, you can make a plan for how to deal with them without turning to food. For example, if you know you tend to eat when you're bored, plan to fill that time with an activity you enjoy, such as reading a book or going for a walk.

2. Suppose you are feeling lonely and bored at home on a Saturday night. You repeatedly find yourself opening the fridge and snacking on chips and cookies, even though you're not physically hungry. To break the cycle of emotional eating, you could try the following: **Identify the triggers**: Ask yourself why you feel lonely and bored. Do you miss social connection? Is there anything else you could do that would make you feel happier? Go out for a walk. Clean the house. Organize the files on your computer.

3. **Find alternative activities**: Instead of turning to food, find other activities that make you feel good. For example, if you feel bored, you can go for a walk, read a book or call a friend or watch a movie. If you feel lonely, you can join a social group or volunteer in your community. Example: Instead of reaching for a bag of chips when you're bored, try going for a walk around the block or calling a friend to talk or join a free seminar or go walk a shelter dog or go out take nature pictures for your blog or organize your home.

4. **Practice mindfulness**: When you have the urge to eat when you're not physically hungry, take a moment to stop and ask yourself how you feel. Acknowledge your feelings without judgment and try to sit with them for a few minutes. You can also try a mindfulness practice like meditation or deep breathing to calm your mind and reduce stress. Or try doing one or all 3 techniques in this book (touching the body, erasing beliefs, page 41).

5. **Have healthy snacks on hand**: If you feel the need to eat, choose healthy snacks such as fruits, vegetables or nuts, such as apple slices with almond butter or thin carrot slices with hummus. Or tea. These foods can help satisfy hunger and provide nutrients that can boost your mood.

6. **Seek support**: If you struggle with emotional eating, consider seeking support from a therapist or support group. They can help you develop healthy coping strategies and provide the emotional support you need.

7. **Find other ways to deal with your feelings**: Instead of turning to food, find other ways to deal with your emotions. For example, if you're feeling stressed, try going for a run or doing yoga. If you feel lonely, call a friend or join a social club to meet new people.

8. **Practice mindfulness**: Mindfulness is the practice of being present in the moment and paying attention to your thoughts and feelings without judgment. When you feel the urge to emotionally eat, try taking a few deep breaths and bringing your attention to the present moment. This can help you resist the urge to eat and deal with your emotions in a more productive way. ***Draw your hunger or write about it (how you feel) or write as if it were your friend and you are talking to each other about it***.

9. **Plan healthy meals and snacks**: Plan ahead and make sure you have healthy meals and snacks on hand. This can prevent you from eating junk food when you're feeling down. For example, if you know you tend to crave sweets when you're stressed, try having some fresh fruit to satisfy your sweet tooth.
Example: Let's say you come home after a long day at work feeling stressed and overwhelmed. Instead of reaching for a bag of chips, try taking a few deep breaths and practicing some relaxation techniques like meditation or yoga. You could also try going for a walk outside or calling a friend to talk about your day or put music shake – dance intense for a while. If you're hungry, plan ahead and have a healthy snack on hand, like a piece of fruit or some raw veggies with hummus. You can break the cycle of emotional eating and feel better both physically and mentally.

10. **Journaling your thoughts and feelings can help you become more aware of what triggers your emotional eating. It can also help you identify patterns in your behavior and develop strategies for dealing with difficult emotions.** It is boring I get it but do you really want a change? Do you?
Example: You notice that you tend to reach for junk food when you feel stressed at work. By journaling, you realize that you feel overwhelmed by your workload and tend to eat as a way to distract yourself from stress. Develop a plan to take short breaks during the workday to practice deep breathing and mindfulness instead of turning to food.

11. **Self-care**: Engaging in self-care activities can help you manage stress and reduce emotional eating. This can include activities such as getting enough sleep, taking a relaxing bath, or spending time with loved ones.
Example: You make sure you get at least 7-8 hours of sleep every night, which helps you feel more rested and better able to handle stressful situations. You

also schedule regular phone calls with friends and family, which gives you an outlet for emotional support. When you take a bath enjoy it with "perfumes" and don't rush to finish it.

12. **Support Groups**: Joining a support group can provide you with a community of people going through similar struggles. This can be helpful in reducing feelings of isolation and shame.
Example: Join a support group for people who struggle with emotional eating. You attend weekly meetings and share your experiences with others who can relate to you. You also get support and encouragement from others on a similar journey.

****

Noticing the steps that are repeated for all these different situations that exist in this book, think if you add these steps into your daily life, how much better your life can become! Since they are important steps to overcome such difficult situations, how positively they will improve your life simply by applying them! You will experience your difficulties with much less intensity and you will see constant changes for the better which is the point after all! **You were not born to suffer!**

****

Selling an e-book online can be a great way to make money if you have valuable content to share. Because we talk about making your suffering or your hobbies in to something creative, I am adding topics like this one to help you spend less time searching for solutions. **Here are some steps you can take to sell your e-book online**:

1. Create an electronic book (E-book): First, you need to write your e-book. Make sure it is well written, informative and **provides value to your readers**.
2. Choose a platform to sell your e-book: You can sell your e-book on your website, through an e-commerce platform like Shopify, or through an online marketplace like Amazon. Each platform has its own pros and cons, so it's important to research each option and choose the one that works best for you.
3. Set a price: You need to set a price for your e-book. Consider the length of your e-book (how many pages), the time and effort you put into creating it, and the value it offers to your readers. You can also research the prices of similar eBooks to get an idea of what the market is offering.
4. Create a page for your book: If you are selling your e-book on your own website, you will need to create a page. This page should be designed to encourage people to buy your e-book. It should include information about your e-book, testimonials from satisfied customers and a call-to-action button.
5. Promote your eBook: Once your eBook is ready to sell, you need to promote it. This can include running ads on social media, reaching out to influencers or

people who have a large audience to promote your e-book (you can give them away and ask them to talk about it) and promoting of via your email list.

6. Order Fulfillment: When someone buys your e-book, make sure you have a system in place to deliver it to them immediately. This can be done automatically through an e-commerce platform or manually via email.

7. Collect feedback: After someone buys and reads your e-book, ask them for feedback. This can help you improve your e-book and provide social proof to potential buyers. Offer those who comment how they liked your book a gift or a great discount to get your first 10-20 comments faster.

8. Tools that can help you sell your e-book online include e-commerce platforms like Shopify and WooCommerce, landing page builders like Leadpages and Unbounce, email marketing platforms like Mailchimp and ConvertKit, and affiliate marketing networks like ShareASale and CJ Affiliate.
Choose a platform (more info below): There are many platforms available for selling e-books online, including Amazon Kindle Direct Publishing, Barnes & Noble Press, Apple iBooks, and Kobo Writing Life. Choose a platform that suits your needs and target audience.

9. Format your e-book: Before uploading your e-book to the platform, you need to format it properly. The platform you choose may have specific formatting requirements, so be sure to check their guidelines.

10. Create a book cover: Your book cover is the first thing readers will see, so make sure it's eye-catching and professional. You can create your own cover using online tools that are free like I do or hire a designer to do it for you.

11. Write a description: Your ebook description should entice readers to buy your book. Write a short, compelling blurb that explains what your book is about and why it's worth reading.

12. When it comes to tools, there are many resources available for formatting, designing, and marketing your e-book. Some popular ones include Canva for book covers (that's what I work on), Reedsy for formatting and design, and BookBub and Goodreads for book promotion.

There are many online platforms where you can upload and sell your e-book with no upfront costs. Some of the popular platforms include:

1. Amazon Kindle Direct Publishing: Amazon KDP allows you to upload and sell your e-book to the Kindle Store. They get a commission from each sale, but there are no upfront costs for publishing.

2. Barnes & Noble Press: This platform allows you to upload and sell your e-book on the Barnes & Noble website. There are no upfront costs, but they get a commission on every sale.

3. Smashwords: Smashwords is an eBook distribution platform that allows you to upload and distribute your eBooks to multiple retailers, including Barnes & Noble, Kobo, and Apple iBooks. They get a commission on every sale, but there are no upfront costs.

4. Kobo Writing Life: Kobo Writing Life is a self-publishing platform that allows you to upload and sell your eBook on the Kobo website. There are no upfront costs, but they get a commission on every sale.

5. Lulu: Lulu is a self-publishing platform that allows you to upload and sell your e-book on their website, as well as to other online retailers. They get a commission on every sale, but there are no upfront costs.

6. Draft2Digital. gumroad.com. www.etsy.com. payhip.com

It is important to note that while there is no upfront cost to publish your e-book on these platforms, you may need to invest in editing, formatting and cover design to make your book attractive to readers.

1. Sell it through your own website: You can create a website or blog and sell your e-book from there. You can use a platform like WordPress or Squarespace to build your website and add an e-commerce plugin like WooCommerce or Shopify to manage payments and product delivery.

2. Use social media: You can leverage your social media accounts to promote and sell your e-book. You can post about your book, share reviews and provide links to where others can buy it.

4. Sell on third-party platforms: There are also several third-party platforms that allow you to sell your e-book online, such as Payhip, Gumroad, and Selz.

5. Offer it as a free download: You can offer your e-book as a free download to build your email list or attract potential customers. You can then sell other products or services to these subscribers.

Remember, no matter which platform you choose, it's important to promote your e-book effectively to maximize sales. This may include leveraging social media, creating promotional materials such as book trailers or blog posts, and reaching out to bloggers or influencers for reviews and suggestions.

1. Selz - Selz is an e-commerce platform that allows you to create a store to sell digital products such as e-books, music, videos and software.

2. E-junkie - E-junkie is a platform that enables you to sell digital products like e-books, music and videos online. It allows you to integrate with popular payment gateways and provide secure download links.

3. Payhip - Payhip is a platform that enables you to sell digital products online. It provides a simple and easy-to-use interface that allows you to create your own digital storefront and start selling your ebooks.

4. Gumroad - Gumroad is a platform that enables creators to sell their digital products online. It provides an easy-to-use interface that allows you to sell eBooks, videos, music and software.

5. Lulu - Lulu is a platform that enables you to self-publish and sell your own ebooks, print books and journals. It also provides tools for formatting and designing your ebook.

And lastly:

1. There are website builders like Wix, Weebly, and WordPress that offer free and paid plans. You can use a payment processing service like PayPal or Stripe to collect payments.

2. Sell on social media: You can use social media platforms like Facebook, Twitter and Instagram to promote and sell your e-book. You can create posts, run ads and use hashtags to attract buyers.

3. There are online marketplaces like Etsy, eBay, and Amazon where you can sell your e-book. These purchases may charge a fee or take a percentage of the sale, so be sure to read the terms and conditions before listing your e-book.

****

Encouraging phrases:

1. Believe in yourself, and in all that you are. Know that there is something within you that is greater than any obstacle.

2. When you feel like giving up, remember why you started.

3. The greatest glory in living is not in never falling, but in getting up every time we fall. -Nelson Mandela.

4. The only way to do great work is to love what you do. -Steve Jobs

5. Success is not final; failure is not fatal: What counts is the courage to continue. -Winston Churchill

6. Don't watch the clock. Keep doing what you're doing.

7. If you want to achieve greatness, stop asking for permission. -Anonymous

8. Life is 10% what happens to you and 90% how you react to it. -Charles R. Swindoll

9. The only place where success comes before work is in the dictionary. -Vidal Sassoon

10. If you want to make your dreams come true, the first thing you have to do is wake up. -J.M. Power

11. Keep your face always towards the sun - and the shadows will fall behind you. -Walt Whitman

12. You miss 100% of the shots you do not do. -Wayne Gretzky

13. A year from now you may wish you had started today. -Karen Lamb

14. Believe you can and you're halfway there. -Theodore Roosevelt

15. I haven't failed. I just found 10,000 ways that won't work. -Thomas Edison

16. It doesn't matter how slow you go as long as you don't stop. -Confucius

17. The best way to predict the future is to create it. - Peter Drucker

18. Success is stumbling from failure to failure without losing enthusiasm. -Winston Churchill

19. Start where you are. Use what you have. Do what you can. - Arthur Ashe

20. The only limit to our realization of tomorrow will be our doubts about today. - Franklin D. Roosevelt

21. The future belongs to those who believe in the beauty of their dreams. - Eleanor Roosevelt

22. Don't let yesterday take you too far from today. -Will Rogers

23. Your time is limited, don't waste it living someone else's life. -Steve Jobs

24. The greatest adventure you can ever have is living the life of your dreams. -Oprah Winfrey

25. If you look at what you have in life, you will always have more. If you look at what you don't have in life, it will never be enough. -Oprah Winfrey

26. The only person you are meant to be is the person you decide to be. -Ralph Waldo Emerson

27. You must be the change you want to see in the world. -Mahatma Gandhi

28. The best revenge is massive success. -Frank Sinatra

29. You deserve the best!

30. Go confidently in the direction of your dreams. Live the life you've dreamed of. - Henry David Thoreau

31. "Every great dream begins with a dreamer. Always remember, you have within you the strength, patience and passion to reach for the stars to change the world."

32. "Success is not measured by what you accomplish, but by the opposition you have encountered and the courage with which you have sustained the struggle against overwhelming odds."

33. "You're never too old to set another goal or dream a new dream."

34. "Believe you can and you're halfway there."

35. "The only way to do great work is to love what you do."

36. "If you can't fly then run, if you can't run then walk, if you can't walk then crawl but whatever you do you have to keep moving".

37. "Believe in yourself, take on your challenges, dig deep to conquer your fears. Never let anyone bring you down."

38. "There are two types of people in this world: those who make things happen and those who watch things happen. Which type are you?"

39. "If you want something you've never had, you have to be willing to do something you've never done."

40. **The only thing standing between you and your goal is the story you keep telling yourself that you can't achieve it**.
41. Everything is learning!
42. "Don't let yesterday take up too much of today." - Will Rogers
43. "What you get by achieving your goals is not as important as what you become by achieving your goals." - Zig Ziglar
44. "You can't change the direction of the wind, but you can adjust your sails so you always reach your destination." - Jimmy Dean
45. **"Motivation is what gets you going. Habit is what keeps you going**." - Jim Rohn
46. "You don't have to be great to start, but you have to start to be great." - Zig Ziglar
47. "Success is not the key to happiness. Happiness is the key to success. If you love what you do, you will be successful." - Albert Schweitzer
48. "The more you read, the more things you'll know. The more you learn, the more places you'll go." - Dr. Seuss
49. "The only way to do great work is to love what you do. If you haven't found it yet, keep looking. Don't settle."

****

The power of persistence.

 Life is not easy, and sometimes we face obstacles that seem insurmountable. But I want to remind you that persistence can overcome almost any obstacle.

When you feel like giving up, remember that the most successful people in the world didn't achieve success overnight. They faced setbacks and failures but never gave up. They persevered and eventually achieved their goals.

So, if you have a dream, if you have a goal that seems impossible, I urge you to persevere. Keep pushing forward, even when you feel like you're not making any progress. And remember, success isn't a destination, it's a journey. So, enjoy the journey and never give up.

Believe in yourself

The power of confidence. You are all capable of achieving great things, but it all starts with believing in yourself.

Don't listen to the naysayers and doubters. Don't let fear hold you back. You have the power to achieve anything you set your mind to, but you have to believe in yourself first.

It won't be easy and there will be times when you doubt yourself. But remember, your thoughts become your reality. If you believe in yourself, you can achieve anything. So, take that first step, believe in yourself and watch life as you make your dreams come true.

****

"The courage to take risks "

Courage to take risks. Life is full of opportunities, but many of them require us to take risks.

It is natural to fear the unknown, to worry about failure. But if we never take risks, we'll never know what we're really capable of.

So, I urge you to have the courage to take a risk. Don't let fear hold you back. Remember, failure is not the opposite of success, it is part of success. You will make mistakes, but you will learn from them and become stronger.

So, take that leap of faith, take that risk, and watch as you accomplish things you never imagined.

****

"The Importance of Gratitude"

In our busy lives, it's easy to take things for granted. But we should never forget how lucky we are.

Take a moment to think about all the good things in your life, all the things that bring you joy and happiness. Even the little things, like a hot cup of coffee on a cold morning or a kind word from a friend. How seeing the sun going up makes you feel.

When we focus on gratitude, we open our hearts and minds to all the good things in the world. We become more positive, more compassionate and more resilient. So, let's all take time to be thankful for the blessings in our lives. There are always good, pleasant moments. We have learned to ignore them and focus only on the bad ones.

"The Power of Teamwork"

When we work together, we can achieve anything. We can overcome any obstacle, face any challenge. And when we succeed, we can celebrate together, as a team. That way we won't feel alone and cut off!

So, let's all remember the importance of teamwork. Let's support each other. Let's encourage each other and work together to achieve our goals.

****

Overcoming adversity

 Life is full of challenges and sometimes it can feel like the world is against us. But it's important to remember that we have the power to overcome any obstacle that comes our way. When we face adversity, it is an opportunity to grow and become stronger. We can use this experience to learn more about ourselves and develop the resilience we need to face future challenges. Remember, the greatest successes often come from the hardest challenges.

****

Pursuit of your dreams

Don't let anyone tell you that your dreams are too big or that you can't achieve them. Chasing your dreams takes courage, dedication and hard work, but it's worth it in the end. Don't let fear or self-doubt stop you from taking action on your goals. Believe in yourself, surround yourself with people who support your dreams and keep moving forward, one step at a time.

****

Living with Purpose

It's easy to fall into the trap of just existing. But true happiness and fulfillment come from living with purpose. Take some time to think about what matters most to you and make it a priority in your life. When we live with purpose, we feel more connected to the world around us and find more meaning and joy in our daily lives.

****

Embracing change

 Change can be scary, but it's also an opportunity for growth and transformation. Don't be afraid to step out of your comfort zone and try new things. Embracing change means opening up to new experiences and opportunities that can help you grow and achieve your goals. Remember, every great achievement begins with a single step. In a change you can meet your loved one or an opportunity of a lifetime!

****

Overcoming fear

Fear can stop us from chasing our dreams and living the life we want. But the truth is that fear is just an emotion and it doesn't have to control us. When we face our fears head on, we realize that we are stronger and more capable than we ever thought we could be. Don't let fear stop you from pursuing your goals and living your best life. Embrace the fear and take action on your dreams.

****

When you're working towards a goal, it's easy to get discouraged and give up when the going gets tough. But the most successful people in the world didn't get where they are by giving up. They persevered in the face of adversity, and so should you.

Think about times in your life when you faced a challenge and wanted to give up. Maybe it was a difficult task at work or a personal struggle. But what if you had just carried on a little longer? What if you had pushed through and kept trying? You may have found that success was just around the corner.

Remember, success is not just about talent or intelligence. It is a matter of persistence and determination. So, keep going, even when the going gets tough. The power of persistence will help you.

****

The truth is that failure is an essential part of the learning process. Every successful person has failed at some point.

The key is to embrace failure and learn from it. When you fail, don't beat yourself up and don't give up. Instead, take a step back and analyze what went wrong. What can you do differently next time? What did you learn from this experience? Did you went up walking in a new path? Did you end up meeting important people? Did you learn how to do something that you never had to deal with before? Why not blog about it and let others know how to do it better!

Remember, failure is not the end of the road. It's just a detour on the road to success. Embrace it, learn from it and keep moving forward. **Life stopped you for your own good. Maybe you were going down the wrong path. Maybe it was the only way for life to show you something great**.

****

Your thoughts have a profound impact on your life, and if you are constantly thinking negative thoughts, it will be difficult to achieve your goals. But if you can learn to think positively, you'll be surprised what you can accomplish.

Start by focusing on what's going on in your life. Even if things aren't perfect, there's always something to be thankful for. And when you are faced with a challenge, try to reframe it in a positive way. Instead of thinking, **"*I can't do this,*" think, *"This is an opportunity to learn and grow."*.**

Remember, your thoughts create your reality. **If you want to be successful, you have to believe that you can be**. So start thinking positive and watch the magic happen.

****

I hope that by repeating – and even if it is written in a different way- some steps, they have begun to take root in you so that you can begin to apply them. The purpose of the book is to help many of you to be filled with joy and happiness by changing the habits that do not help you but they harm you. I hope I can do that to some of you! It is like reading the book more than once by reading some steps more than once!

****

It's easy to get caught up in the demands of everyday life and forget to take care of ourselves. But the truth is, if you don't prioritize your own well-being, you'll struggle to be your best self.

Self-care looks different for everyone, but it can include things like taking a relaxing bath, going for a walk in nature, or meditating or listening to your music or enjoying you tea looking at the sun going up or daydreaming of how you want your life to be. Whatever helps you feel refreshed and happy. Make time for this on a regular basis. Especially on difficult and demanding days. Don't forget to see and do things that make you laugh a lot!!

Remember, self-care is not selfish. Is necessary. When you take care of yourself, you can take better care of others and face life's challenges with a clear mind and positive attitude.

****

Here are some common negative phrases and ways to rephrase them in a positive way:

1. **Negative**: "I hate Mondays." **Positive**: "I look forward to finding joy in every day, including Mondays».
2. **Negative**: "I can't do that." **Positive**: "I can do anything I put my mind to. I'm going to break it down into smaller steps to make it easier and more fun».

3. **Negative**: "This is very difficult." **Positive**: "This is a challenge, but I am capable of overcoming any obstacle».

4. **Negative**: "I don't have enough time." **Positive**: "I have enough time to complete everything I need to do today. I manage my time effectively».

5. **Negative**: "I'm not good enough." **Positive**: "I am constantly growing and improving and have many strengths and talents to offer».

6. **Negative**: "I'm so stressed." **Positive**: "I am able to manage my stress and find peace within myself."

7. **Negative**: "I hate my job." **Positive**: "I am grateful for the opportunity to work and learn new skills. I'm taking steps to find work that better aligns with my passions and interests."

8. **Negative**: "I'm so fat and ugly." **Positive**: "I am beautiful and worthy of love and I make healthy choices every day to take care of my body."

9. **Negative**: "I'm not lucky." **Positive**: "I am grateful for all the blessings in my life and create my own luck through everything I do, with positivity and determination."

10. **Negative**: "I don't have enough money." **Positive**: "I am grateful for the abundance in my life and I am taking steps to properly manage my finances and create a life of abundance and prosperity."

11. **Negative**: "I can't do it" **Positive**: "I can do it if I try"

12. **Negative**: "I'm not good enough" **Positive**: "I'm always improving and learning"

13. **Negative**: "I'll never be able to figure it out" **Positive**: "I haven't figured it out yet, but I'll keep trying"

14. **Negative**: "I hate Mondays" **Positive**: "I'm grateful for the new week and the opportunities it brings"

15. **Negative**: "I'm so stressed" **Positive**: "I'm able to handle challenges and find solutions"

16. **Negative**: "I have to do this" **Positive**: "I choose to do this because it aligns with my goals and values"

17. **Negative**: "I'm too busy" **Positive**: "I prioritize my time and focus on what's important"

18. **Negative**: "I'm so unlucky" **Positive**: "I create my own opportunities and attract positive outcomes"

19. **Negative**: "I can't believe this happened to me" **Positive**: "I have the strength and endurance to overcome any obstacle"

20. **Negative**: "I will never be able to forgive myself" **Positive**: "I learn from my mistakes and grow as a person full of wisdom"

21. **Negative**: "I can't do that." **Positive**: "I'll give it my best and we'll see what happens."

22. **Negative**: "I hate Mondays." **Positive**: "I'm grateful for the opportunity to start this new week."

23. **Negative**: "I'm so stressed." **Positive**: "I'm feeling a little overwhelmed right now, but I know I can handle it."

24. **Negative**: "I'll never be as good as [someone else]." **Positive**: "I may not be [someone else], but I have my own unique talents and strengths to offer."

25. **Negative**: "Nothing ever goes right for me." **Positive**: "I've had some setbacks, but I know things will change if I keep moving forward."

26. **Negative**: "I'm so bad at [something]." **Positive**: "I'm still learning and getting better at [something]."

27. **Negative**: "I'm so tired." **Positive**: "Could give me more rest but it's something I can easily overcome. However, I always take good care of myself."

28. **Negative**: "I'll never do it all." **Positive**: "I have a lot to do, but I can take it one step at a time."

29. **Negative**: "I'm so unlucky." **Positive**: "I am grateful for all the good things in my life and look forward to more positive experiences."

30. **Negative**: "I'm not good enough." **Positive**: "I'm enough just the way I am, and I'll keep getting wiser and better."

✱✱✱✱✱✱✱✱✱✱✱✱✱✱✱✱✱✱✱✱✱✱

Funny motivational phrases to brighten your day:

1. «I've always wanted to be somebody, but now I realize I should have been more specific." - Lily Tomlin
2. "Procrastination is like a credit card: it's great fun until you get the bill." - Christopher Parker
3. "I'm so smart that sometimes I don't understand a word of what I'm saying." - Oscar Wilde

4. "I haven't failed. I've just found 10,000 ways that won't work. Don't worry, I'll find you more"
5. "I find that the harder I work, the luckier I seem to get." - Thomas Jefferson
6. "If you don't succeed at first, then skydiving is definitely not for you." - Steven Wright
7. "Don't bother me now, I'm upgrading come later." - Jimmy Dean
8. " I'm not great at advice. Would you mind a sarcastic comment?" - Chandler Bing (from friends)
9. "I'm not lazy, I'm just keeping my energy up."
10. "Procrastination is just a fancy word for 'being busy doing nothing.'
11. " I can do anything, but not forever. That's what coffee is for. It's my battery I need you to feed me every day "
12. "I'm not arguing, just explaining why I'm right."
13. "I don't always have a plan, but when I do, it's bad."
14. "I have a personality you can't handle, but also a face you can't resist."
15. "The only thing standing between me and success is me...and maybe a little procrastination".

****

What to do when someone is angry with you:

1. **Start breakdancing**: Sometimes, all you need to diffuse a tense situation is a little dance. Do some funky moves to lighten the mood.
2. **Make funny faces**: Stick out your tongue, cross your eyes. It's hard to stay angry when someone makes silly faces at you.

3. **Offer them a snack**: Maybe they're just hungry! Offer a tasty treat to help them refuel and hopefully feel better.

4. **Hug Them**: It's hard to stay angry when you're wrapped in a warm hug. Just make sure the other person feels okay if you touch them!

5. **Suggest a tickle match**: If they're really angry, they might not like this, but if they're open to it, a tickle match can be a great way to lighten the mood and get a laugh.

6. **Tell a joke**: It can do wonders to break the ice and reduce tension. Just make sure it's the right fit!

7. **Make them laugh** with a funny video: Send them something funny from the internet to make them smile.

8. **Do a silly dance**: The sillier the better.

9. **Suggest doing something fun together**: Maybe they just need a distraction from whatever is making them angry.

10. **Apologize and offer to make amends**. Sometimes the best thing to do is to sincerely apologize and offer to make amends.

11. Show up on their doorstep with a **cake that says 'I'm sorry'**.

12. Buy them a new **houseplant** as a peace offering.

13. **Write** them a heartfelt letter of **apology**.

14. Show up at their workplace when they're done in a **ridiculous outfit** (as a clown, dinosaur or unicorn, etc.) and ask if they can forgive you for your ridiculous behavior.

****

Setting boundaries is an essential part of maintaining healthy relationships. **Here are some suggestions on how to set boundaries with different people in your life**:

To set boundaries effectively, it's important to be clear and direct in your communication. Use "I" statements to express your needs and concerns and **be specific** about what behaviors are and are not acceptable. Remember that setting boundaries isn't about controlling others, it's about making sure you're respected and valued.

You can also use tools like journaling, therapy, or self-help books to help you clarify your boundaries and develop the skills to communicate them effectively. Remember that setting boundaries is a process and it may take time and practice to become comfortable with it. But with patience and persistence, you can create healthy, fulfilling relationships with those around you.

1. If your child does not respect you or others, you may need to set limits on his behavior, such as taking away privileges (cell phone, internet, walks, the computer, etc.). **You should not punish a behavior in general** but be specific and say exactly what behavior is not acceptable without labeling it. Example: Interrupting……makes the other person feel…… would you like to be interrupted? If you do it again I will take away your privilege…… (no you're an ass, a coward, you're embarrassing me, get out of here….etc..). If you have children, it's important to set clear boundaries around their behavior and your expectations. For example, you can set rules about how they treat others, how they use technology, and how they communicate with you. You can also set

consequences for breaking these rules that you will apply. **Do not just say them but never apply them**. Does your child interrupt you while you are on a phone conversation? You can set a boundary by calmly explaining to your child that you are on an important call and that he must wait until you finish and put them to do something. You can also before starting the call give them something to do during this time, like coloring something or reading a book.

2. If a friend is constantly canceling plans at the last minute, you **may need to let them know that this behavior is not acceptable and is causing you stress**. If he keeps it up you won't choose to make any plans with him even if you are having such a great time with him when you finally manage to meet.

3. If a family member is constantly asking you for money or expecting you to help with their problems, you may need to set boundaries around whether: you will lend to them again and what else you should do. Example: Or asking and taking something as a guarantee that he will return it to you. Or spend a lot less time helping him from here on out. Or let him do it himself now and then to force himself to learn to find solutions.

4. If your partner makes you feel uncomfortable or doesn't respect your boundaries, you may need to talk to them about their behavior and set clear expectations about how you expect them to treat you. Example: Your partner is constantly late for appointments: You can set a boundary by telling your partner that you value punctuality and that being late makes you anxious. You can suggest that they set a reminder on their phone or that you set it, or that they make a plan to be on time. If they don't, tell them you'll stop wanting to date them since they always make you wait or forget to come. (This is disrespectful and again think about whether this person is worth being with.)

5. Your friend keeps asking you for loans: You can set a boundary by **being honest** with your friend and **letting him know that you don't feel comfortable** lending him money all the time. **You can suggest other ways in which you can help** them, like helping them find a job or something else depending on why they keep asking you for money.

6. A relative makes critical comments about your appearance: You can set a boundary by telling your family member that you don't appreciate their comments and that they make you feel uncomfortable. You can also suggest that they keep their comments to themselves in the future. You can say that you will stop going and also invite him to your house if he behaves like this.

7. Your coworker consistently takes credit for your work: You can set a boundary by **speaking up** and letting your coworker know that you don't appreciate their

behavior. You can also document (record the steps you take or that you do it) your work and give your boss the record to ensure you get credit for your efforts.

8. Your neighbor often invites himself unannounced: You can set a boundary by politely letting your neighbor know that they need to notify you before coming over. You can suggest that they call or text you ahead of time to see if it's a good time to visit. If they keep doing it, don't let them in, say that is a bad time, you didn't call me first, I can't because: you're cleaning the house, you got ready to take a bath, you're getting ready to go out, etc. And **close the door on him**.

9. In a group chat with friends or family, if someone starts talking over you or interrupts you, you can say something like, "I'm sorry, I'd like to finish my thought" or "Can I talk without being interrupted!"

10. If someone asks you for a favor that you don't feel comfortable doing or that would be inconvenient for you, it's okay to say no. You can say something like, "I'm sorry, but I can't do that right now" or "I can't help you with that".

11. A therapist can help you identify and set boundaries and develop strategies for maintaining them.

12. There are many books available that provide guidance on setting and maintaining boundaries. Some popular titles: "Boundaries" by Henry Cloud and John Townsend and "The Assertiveness Guide for Women" by Julie de Azevedo Hanks.

13. Role-playing exercises: Practicing setting and maintaining boundaries through role-playing exercises, can help you feel more confident and prepared in real-life situations.

14. Support groups: Joining a support group can give you a community of people who are also working on setting and maintaining boundaries. **You will be able to exchange strategies and ideas**.

****

Dealing with someone who constantly creates arguments can be challenging, but there are a few strategies you can use to try to diffuse the situation and stop the fighting.

1. **Actively listen**: When someone is arguing with you, it can be easy to get defensive and stop listening. However, actively listening to the other person's point of view can help de-escalate the situation. **Repeat back what they said** to you to show that you understand and are trying to listen.
Examples:
"If I understand correctly, you say you feel your contributions to the project have gone unrecognized. Is that so?"

"It sounds like you're frustrated because you feel like you're not being heard. Am I right?"

"Let me make sure I follow up with you—you're concerned that we're not putting enough resources into this initiative. Is that what you're trying to tell me?"

2. **Avoid responding emotionally**: It can be tempting to react emotionally and respond with anger or frustration. However, responding with emotions can often make the situation worse. Try to stay calm and answer rationally.

   Examples:

   "I understand you're upset, but please let's keep our conversation respectful. We're both here to find a solution."

   "I can see we have different opinions on this, and that's fine. Let's try to find some common ground and go from there."

   "I appreciate your passion on this issue, but let's focus on the facts and try to find a solution that works for everyone involved."

3. **Set boundaries**: If someone is constantly trying to argue with you, it's important to set boundaries and let them know that **their behavior is not acceptable**. This can help avoid arguments in the future.

   Examples:

   Tell him that you don't feel comfortable chatting with him about the topic he keeps arguing about every time you talk about it.

   "I understand that you have a strong opinion on this matter, but please don't talk down to me or try to start an argument every time we talk about it."

   "I'm happy to have a conversation with you, but I won't engage in name-calling or insults. If you can't speak to me respectfully, then we won't be able to have a productive conversation."

   "I appreciate your input, but if we can't have a constructive discussion without it turning into an argument, then **I'll have to end the discussion here and leave**".

   Don't start this topic because each time you do you end up talking very upsetting. **If you keep it up, I will leave. I am not here to hear you talk like this. I came to have a good time with you**.

4. **Walk away**: If someone is being particularly aggressive or the argument is getting out of hand, it may be best to **just walk away from the situation**. This can help de-escalate the situation and prevent it from getting worse. Go away. Change room or leave the area where the fight is taking place. Get out there and keep walking.

5. **Get professional help**: If you're dealing with someone who is constantly arguing and it's affecting your mental health, it may be helpful to seek professional help if you can't get them out of your life. A therapist can give you tools and strategies to manage the condition and protect your well-being.

1. "I see your point, but I see things differently".
2. " Can we take a break and come back to this later when we're both calmer?"
3. "Let's try to find a solution that works for both of us".
4. " I don't think it's productive for us to argue like that. Can we try to have a constructive discussion?"
5. " I'm sorry if I said something that upset you. Can we discuss this calmly?"
6. "I understand where you're coming from, but let's try to find a solution that works for both of us."
7. " I see this is important to you. Let's take a break and come back to it when we're both calmer."
8. " I don't want to argue with you. Let's focus on finding a solution."
9. " I don't agree with you, but I respect your opinion. Can we find a compromise?"
10. "I hear what you're saying, but let's approach this with kindness and understanding."
11. "Let's take a step back and try to see things from the other person's perspective."
12. " I don't think we get anywhere by arguing. Let's find a way to move forward ".
13. "I care about you and our relationship. Let's work together to find a solution".
14. " Can we just agree to disagree and move on from this?"

****

An email list can be a powerful asset to any business or organization. It allows you to communicate directly with your audience, build relationships and promote your products or services. **Here are some ways to leverage your email list to grow your business**:

1. **Send newsletters regularly without overdoing it**: Newsletters are a great way to keep your audience informed about your business or organization. Promote your products or services as well as valuable content that your audience will find useful. But don't send every day, let it be once a week or 1-2 times a month. For example, an e-commerce store might send a promotional email

with a discount code for a new product, while a restaurant might send an email with a special holiday menu. A marketing agency might send out a newsletter with tips on how to improve your social media strategy, while a nonprofit might send out a newsletter with stories about the impact of their work.

2. **Build relationships**: Your email list is also an opportunity to build relationships with your audience. You can use your emails to deliver value and build trust with your subscribers, which can lead to long-term loyalty. For example, a real estate agent might send a monthly email with home maintenance tips, while a gym might send a weekly email with workout tips and motivation to stay fit.

3. **Segment your list**: Segmenting your email list allows you to send targeted messages to specific groups of subscribers. For example, you can segment your list by location, interests, or behavior. This allows you to send more personalized messages that are relevant to your audience. For example, a clothing seller might send a promotional email featuring winter coats to subscribers in cold climates, while sending summer dresses to subscribers in warmer climates.

4. **Use automation**: Email automation allows you to send targeted messages at the right time without having to manually send each message. This may include welcome emails, abandoned cart reminders and post-purchase follow-up. For example, an e-commerce store might send a series of emails to new subscribers, including a welcome email, a discount code, and a follow-up email a week later.

5. **Conduct surveys**: Surveys are a great way to get feedback from your audience and learn more about their needs and interests. You can use surveys to solicit feedback about your products or services, to gather ideas for new content or products, or simply to get to know your audience better. For example, a software company might send out a survey to ask for feedback on a new feature, while a nonprofit might send out a survey to gather feedback about its programs and services.

6. **Personalize your messages**: Personalization can improve the effectiveness of email marketing by making your messages more relevant and engaging. You can personalize your emails using your subscriber's first name, including product recommendations based on their past purchases or by sending content tailored to their interests. For example, a retailer can send a personalized email with a discount code for a product the subscriber has

shown interest in, while a publisher can send an email with recommended articles based on the subscriber's reading history.

7. **Provide exclusive content**: Offering exclusive content to your email subscribers can help build loyalty and keep your audience engaged. This may include early access to new products or services, exclusive discounts or special events. For example, a fashion retailer might offer early access to a new clothing line to its email subscribers, while a software company might offer a free webinar to its subscribers.

8. **Use social proof**: Social proof is a powerful way to influence people's behavior and encourage them to take action. You can use social proof in your email marketing by including customer reviews, testimonials, or user-generated content. For example, a travel company might include customer reviews of a destination in its email marketing, while an e-commerce store might include user-generated photos of its products.

****

Prioritization, here are some ways you can approach the process of prioritization:

Determine your values: The first step in setting priorities is to determine what is most important to you. This can be done by thinking about and writing down your values and what you want to achieve in life. For example, if you value family above all else, then spending time with loved ones may be your top priority.

Health: Health is important to many people as it affects their quality of life and ability to carry out daily activities.

Education: Many people see education as a very important tool for developing their skills and achieving their career goals.

Social relationships: Creating and maintaining social relationships with other people is important to many people, as this can enhance their well-being and happiness, etc.

Create a list: Once you've identified your values, make a list of all the things you need to do. This may include tasks related to your work, personal goals and other obligations. Writing down your to-dos can help you see the bigger picture and prioritize more easily.

Example: If you put health first, there are a few things you can do every day to improve and maintain your health:

1. Eat healthy: Consume a rich, varied diet that includes lots of fruits, vegetables, whole grains, healthy proteins, and less processed foods and sugar.

2. Exercise daily: Take at least 30 minutes a day to exercise, walking, running, swimming, yoga or other aerobic exercises. Monday walk. Tuesday swimming pool. Wednesday walking etc.

3. Drink enough water: At least 2 liters of water a day to keep my body hydrated. Etc.

Wednesday shopping at the market. Saturday laundries etc.

Consider urgency and importance: Urgent tasks may require your immediate attention, but important tasks may have a more significant impact on your overall goals. For example, paying bills may be urgent, but investing in your education may be more important in the long run.

Use a ranking system: To make prioritization easier, assign a ranking to each task on your list. For example, use a scale of 1 to 5, with 1 being the least important and 5 being the most important. This can help you quickly see which tasks require your attention first.

Be realistic: It's important to be realistic about what you can accomplish in a given day or week. Trying to tackle too many tasks can lead to burnout and overwhelm. Instead, prioritize the most important tasks and give yourself enough time to complete them.

Reassess regularly: Priorities can change over time, so it's important to regularly reassess your list and adapt it to your needs. This can help you stay focused on what is most important to you.

Here are some examples of how you can use these strategies:

Example 1: Values: Health, Career, Family

List: Go to the gym. Attending a conference for work. Attending a family gathering. Completion (that something) for your work. Cooking a healthy meal.

Here are some examples of how you can use these strategies:

Priority: Attend work conference (5), Complete work project (4), Cook a healthy meal (3), Go to the gym (2), Attend a family gathering (1).

Example 2: Values: Education, Relationships, Personal Development

List: Study for exams. Go to the appointment. Attend a networking event. Take yoga classes. Volunteer at a local organization.

Priority: Study for the exam (5), Attend the networking event (4), Volunteer at a local organization (3), Sign up for a yoga class (2), Go on the date (1).

Use the Eisenhower Matrix: The Eisenhower Matrix is a useful tool that can help you prioritize tasks based on their urgency and importance. This tool divides tasks into four categories: important and urgent, important but not urgent, urgent but not important and not important and not urgent. This can help you quickly determine which tasks require immediate attention and which can be delegated or delayed. Example:

Values: Work, Health, Relationships

List: Complete a work project. Schedule an appointment with a doctor. Have lunch with a friend. Respond to non-urgent emails. Clean the house.

Priority: Complete the work project (important and urgent). Schedule a doctor's appointment (important but not urgent). Have lunch with a friend (not urgent but important). Respond to non-urgent emails (urgent but not important). Clean the house (not important and not urgent).

Otherwise make lists with paper and pen in a similar pattern.

Consider the Consequences: When setting priorities, it is important to consider the consequences of not completing certain tasks. For example, not completing a work project on time could affect your career prospects. If you don't take care of your health, you may develop chronic health problems later on. This can help you put things in perspective and prioritize accordingly.

Break your tasks into smaller ones: Sometimes, tasks can seem overwhelming, which can make it difficult to prioritize. In these cases, it can be helpful to break tasks down into smaller, more manageable steps. For example, if your goal is to write a book, you can break it down into tasks such as outlining chapters, researching, and writing that many pages in a set amount of time each day (Example: 5 pages each day).

Use a calendar or organizer: Using a calendar or organizer can help you stay organized and keep track of deadlines. You can set aside specific hours and days of your time for tasks and appointments, which can help you prioritize your time more effectively.

Here's an example of how you can use these strategies:

Values: Personal Development, Career, Relationships

List: Write a blog post. Attend a networking event. Take a foreign language course. Have dinner with a friend. Read a professional development book.

Priority: Attend networking event (important and urgent), Write a blog post (important but not urgent), Take a language class (not urgent but important), Have dinner with a friend (not important but urgent), Read a professional development book (not important and not urgent).

Pareto Principle: The Pareto Principle, also known as the 80/20 rule, suggests that 80% of the results come from 20% of the effort. This can be applied to prioritizing by focusing on the tasks that will have the greatest impact on your goals. For example, if you are a salesperson, you can focus on the 20% of customers that generate 80% of your sales.

Mind Mapping: Mind Mapping is a technique that can help you visually organize your thoughts and ideas. It involves creating a diagram that starts with a central idea and branches out into related ideas and subtopics. This can help you identify the most important tasks and prioritize them based on their relationship to your central goal.

ABC Method: The ABC method involves categorizing tasks as A, B or C based on their importance. A tasks are the most important and urgent, B tasks are important but not urgent, and C tasks are neither important nor urgent. This can help you quickly identify tasks that require your immediate attention if the above seem like time-consuming processes.

Time Blocking: Time blocking involves scheduling specific chunks of time for tasks and activities. This can help you prioritize your time and ensure you have enough time to complete important tasks. For example, you can block the hours 9-11am. to complete a work project, 12-1 p.m. for exercise and 2-3 p.m. to reply to emails.

For more humor and fun color, the tasks or the boxes in which you will write the corresponding tasks.

The Ivy Lee Method: The Ivy Lee Method is a simple technique that involves identifying the six most important tasks for the day and ranking them in order of importance. Then you focus on completing each task one at a time until they are all done. This can help you stay focused and avoid getting distracted by less important tasks.

Here's an example of how you can use these tools:

Values: Health, Personal Development, Career

List: Exercise for 30 minutes, attend a leadership training seminar, call a client, schedule a doctor's appointment, update your resume.

Priority: Attend leadership training (A), schedule a doctor's appointment (A), call a client (B), update your resume (B), exercise for 30 minutes (C).

****

Prioritizing customer needs is vital for any business as it helps ensure customer satisfaction, which leads to repeat business and referrals. Here are some ways to prioritize customer needs:

Identify your customer needs: The first step in prioritizing customer needs is to determine what they are. You can do this by conducting market research, analyzing customer feedback and monitoring social media channels. For example, if you own a coffee shop, you can conduct a survey to find out what types of drinks, coffees your customers prefer.

Categorize your customers: Once you've identified your customers' needs, you can categorize them based on their level of importance. For example, you can categorize your customers as high priority, medium priority and low priority based on their spending (shopping) habits or frequency of visits.

Respond to Urgent Needs First: It is important to respond to urgent customer needs first to prevent any negative consequences. For example, if a customer is not satisfied with their order, it is important to address the problem immediately to prevent them from leaving a negative review or telling others about their bad experience.

Prioritize repeat (frequent shopper) customers: Repeat customers are the lifeblood of any business and it is important to prioritize their needs to ensure they continue to do business (buy) with you. This may include offering personalized services, remembering their preferences and providing special offers and discounts based on their preferences.

Offer customized solutions: One way to prioritize customer needs is to offer customized solutions that meet their specific needs. For example, if a customer is looking for a gluten-free menu, you can offer them a custom menu with gluten-free options. And if you don't have, there it is an opportunity to provide a service that you didn't have!

Anticipate future needs: It is important to anticipate the future needs of your customers and be ready to meet them. This may include introducing new products or services, forecasting seasonal demand, and providing training and support to help customers get the most out of your products or services.

Here are some examples of how these suggestions can be applied in different industries:

Restaurant: A restaurant can prioritize regular customers or high-spending customers by offering them personalized service, knowing their preferences and providing them with special offers and discounts. It can also prioritize urgent needs, such as dealing with complaints or issues with orders, to prevent negative reviews. The restaurant can also offer customized solutions such as creating a menu with gluten-free options and anticipate future needs by introducing new seasonal menus or offering cooking classes or do a cooking competition.

Retail: A retailer can prioritize high-priority customers by offering them a loyalty program or personalized shopping experiences and tips on how to use their products. For example: If they have clothes give tips on how to combine them to slim your body. It can also respond to urgent needs, such as addressing complaints or product issues, and offer customized solutions, such as providing customized product recommendations based on customer preferences. The store can anticipate future needs by introducing new products or services and providing training and support to help customers get the most out of their purchases. And by making the complains in to new products or in to new tips.

Healthcare: A healthcare provider can prioritize urgent needs, such as addressing medical issues or patient concerns, to provide timely and effective care. It may also prioritize repeat patients by offering personalized services and remembering their medical history and preferences. The provider can offer personalized solutions, such as creating treatment plans that meet patients' specific needs and concerns, and anticipating future needs by introducing new treatments or technologies and providing education and resources to help patients manage their health.

Mapping the customer journey can help you identify pain points and areas where you can improve the customer experience. By understanding the steps customers take when interacting with your business, you can prioritize improvements that will have the biggest impact.

Net Promoter Score (NPS): NPS is a tool that measures customer loyalty by asking customers how likely they are to recommend your business to others. By tracking your NPS score over time, you can prioritize improvements that will help increase customer loyalty and satisfaction.

Gathering customer feedback through surveys or other means can help you understand their needs and preferences. By prioritizing comments that are most relevant or mentioned most often, you can focus your efforts on the areas that matter most to your customers.

****

1. «I'm doing my best and that's all that matters»

2. «I am worthy of love and respect»

3. «I'm proud of myself for trying»

4. «I am confident in my abilities»

5. «I am in control of my thoughts and actions»

6. «I am grateful for all the good things in my life»

7. «I am capable of achieving my goals»

8. «I am unique and special just the way I am»

9. «I am surrounded by people who love and support me»

10. «It is not part of my reality to be sick because I do not choose illness for myself».

11. «Sickness, poverty, pain is no longer part of my reality. »

12. «I attract everything I need»

****

People often become vulnerable when they don't feel well. They feel incredibly tired all the time, causing them to grow desperate and seek relief. Desperation according to experts paves the way for the logic of "what have I got to lose I'll try, no matter what and being like this is not the best". It is some kind of motivation.

****

Every new day is the first day of the rest of your life!

****

Empty your house of broken things making space in your life! Yes! By emptying the trash from our house, we will immediately feel as if we made room in our life for joy, new things and we will love our space again! **Don't keep things you forgot you had them for 3 long years!** Do not stuff the wardrobes inside and out, above the wardrobe in the space it has and below in the middle. **Don't fill your space with a bunch of stuff**. Keep your space as organized and light as possible. Give away what's not broken but you don't need and recycle what's broken! Let the positive energy flow calmly in your home and in your life! Get rid of unnecessary weight!

****

Get up and put on soft music and let your body move as it pleases. Enjoy it! And if you have children, try it together! You unwind and relax from stress and a sedentary lifestyle. You forget the problems for a while by doing that and you do something good for you! You get rid of everything even if it is for a while! Try it without judging yourself by saying "What nonsense am I doing now......»!

****

Einstein said: "There are 2 ways to live. One is as if there are no miracles, and the other is as if everything is a miracle." Life itself, nature, our planet, our existence, all are miracles! See your every moment as a miracle! And you will see wonderful changes pop up all around you!

****

There are always more options than most people realize, even when it seems like you've reached a dead end. Everything that happens in our lives is a result of our thoughts and reactions, and we participate in them actively and with our consent. It is important to accept this fact and realize that you have the power to change your situation, since you yourself created it with your thoughts and actions.

****

The negative behavior or qualities you observe in other people may be something that bothers you in yourself. It's important to explore those parts of yourself that you don't like, find their roots and understand how they affect your life.

****

An example of how a fear, a false belief, can be created: In your childhood, one of your parents or your siblings or someone very close to you suffered from some health problem. You see him suffering and you are filled with the fear "never find myself in pain like this or never find myself suffering from this...". You may be thinking "maybe it's something hereditary and I will get it too?" And then, as a survival mechanism, you decide, for example, that when you grow up, you will remove the entire part of the instrument so that you will never suffer like this. Or from now on you are afraid of getting sick, etc. Your opinion about the organ, the situation, the pain, became a phobia, became a useless belief, drawing your own conclusions from the whole situation. Many of our worries we don't even know how they were created. But we know how they scare us and keep us inactive. You now have ways to disable them. Try as the techniques written in this book. See which one suits you!

****

Maybe it's time to realize that we don't know everything and we are constantly learning from everything! Even from the children! Learn to say " **You may be right! I don't know why things are the way they are, someone at some point said this is the way it should be done and this is done without anyone asking why we do it this**

even way..." it does not mean that you have failed if you say it or that you are not enough. It's not a bad thing to say it.

The bad thing is to act like we know it all and get annoyed with the different opinions of others. The bad thing is to get angry and not be able to discuss calmly, with arguments and saying when necessary "**I have no idea……. I never thought of it that way**………. it doesn't matter if you or I are right we each have our own opinions and we are just having a conversation….».

 Let's listen even more to the children who can still see life as beautiful and can awaken us to see it like this again.

****

No need to be poor, sick, in pain, etc. Say no more pain! No more poverty! Wake up!

****

Why do you still keep the pain, the misery, the……… in your life?

****

Who said things have to be so hard and if they aren't they aren't worth having?

****

Why do we remain so trapped in our pain, in our need to say and feel that we are "fighting" everyday?

****

Why don't we accept with the same ease and happiness that is clearly in front of us?

****

Every day we have the same choice: To take whatever comes our way the hard way or the easy way. But we choose the hard way again and again.

****

Start each day thinking positively:

I feel great!

I feel full of excitement!

I feel strong!

I feel happy!

I look like an interesting person!

I'm beautiful!

I am releasing everything I no longer need!

I easily attract everything I want and need!

Say them with joy and enthusiasm and with a smile and when you are out somewhere and you are bored or have a bad feeling start saying them in you! Leave, say you have to go get something to eat or ……… change the environment and say such positive words from within! Go to the toilet so you don't get seen, look in the mirror and with a smile say it from the inside making winning moves! React creatively and positively!

****

Don't just hope for something! Convince yourself that you did it! **Think you've got it**! Whatever it is, health, appearance, freedom, money... Don't spend your time thinking and saying, in various ways, **that you don't have it**. Don't talk about it anymore! Go home and walk in, jump for joy as if you have it and find time to **envision, make a picture of your life as it is because you have It**. Sit in your car and think about it, picture your life as it is because you have it! While you are taking a bath, think about it and make movements of joy because you have it! Be careful not to slip:PPPp!

****

Ask yourself which part of you has the wants and needs you listed as goals. Do you think it comes from the past? Does it stem from the past, because of the lack of material goods you had from back then? Does the child in you want it, does it need it? Does your adult self-need it? Do that to all of your goals, need and wants.

****

You are not condemned to live as a prisoner of your emotions. When you feel bad look inside yourself find why and decide to deal with it immediately. Don't let it take root. Try the ideas suggested in this book. You deserve to smile!

****

If you have reached the point where your days flow indifferently and you have forgotten what gives you joy or you often suffer from headaches and various pains, negative emotions, etc. Start doing something for yourself every day, day after day. Something that pleases you and something that relaxes you. To start experiencing a better everyday life again.

****

I'M RELEASING EVERYTHING I DON'T NEED ANYMORE!!! Say it many times! Especially as you fall asleep!

****

What is the essence of the problem?
What does this situation offer me?
What are the positive consequences?
Is pain, illness an occasion to devote time and attention to myself?
Write your answers.

****

Stop saying "I'm fine but……. Or I'm fine now but…" There is no but! **But** attracts negative events!

****

Go to a doctor or visit someone in hospital or at home where they are recovering. Think positively that **you are visiting a place of healing where wonderful things can happen, not a place of disease**!

****

We are so full of our old thoughts and experiences that we leave no room to see anything with new eyes. This fills us with boredom, with negative feelings, with the feeling that we do not know what we want in our lives. Why choose to remain unhappy?

****

Ask yourself:

What meaning, purpose, value does this move have for you now?

What effect will it have on your next move?

How do you assess the overall situation?

How can you improve it?

……. **also ask the above questions to understand the situation you are in**.

****

One more problem-solving technique and understanding:

First you need to identify the problem.

Second step is to record the emotions that the problem causes.

Step three is to list and evaluate your options for solving the problem.

Fourth step is to look at the whole thing as a whole. With all 3 steps combined.

The last step is to implement the existing solutions. (Do you have better things to do than deal with it and be emotionally invested in it?)

****

Let's say you have a cast on your leg or for some reason you have to cancel something and stay at home for a while. Ask yourself: What can I do for the next 6 weeks that I couldn't otherwise do? And do it! Enjoy this time instead of staying angry!

****

You feel anger and a lot of bad feelings for someone. **Take a paper and write them down**. Keep the letter for 3 days and see if your anger has calmed down a bit. In this letter, write what you feel. Analyze why you feel this way. **Also write what the solutions are**. If you don't feel calmer after 3 days, send your letter. If you have calmed down or you no longer feel the need to express your indignation, burn the letter.

****

If the solutions all seem bad to you, choose **the least bad one**.

****

If someone or something offends you, hurts you in some way, you are offended yourself, you are hurting yourself. Since nothing can hurt you like a physical hurt, then you decide to feel hurt (by a painting, by another's words, etc.). You then unfairly blame others. This nonsense is not personal to you! So why do you want to be offended? Why do you need to feel this way? Why do you need to feel wronged? Why don't you see the situation as funny?

People looking for reasons to be offended will always find a reason to feel that way.

****

In life there is unhappiness because we create it. Unhappiness just doesn't happen like that. So why are you unhappy? Find why and solve it!

****

Would I want everyone who is and will be in my position to act like me? If not then why am I doing this?

****

Nature intended that we will not need special equipment to live happily! Each of us is capable of making our own happiness. Objects hold us captive. What matters cannot be taken from you because it is within you.

****

Society shapes us, but at some point we have to take responsibility for what habits we develop.

****

Commitment is not a loss of freedom but an exercise of freedom. There is always an exit (break up) that you simply choose not to use.

****

By sharing power, you can draw strength from a relationship rather than expending all energy maintaining dominance. A well maintained relationship becomes an energy generator, a source of clean, safe and abundant energy. **We should not treat others as means to our own ends. We should appreciate them as people with their own purposes**. Be selfish wisely. Care for the end as well as the beginning and you will never fail.

****

Home is not only where your heart is and where you should be accepted (which you may not be accepted). Home is where people listen to you carefully and are interested in your thoughts and feelings. It is where you are treated as a human being with values and expectations, without hidden agendas, appreciating you for who you are.

****

A couple can live a beautiful relationship and exchange wedding vows while growing as individuals. However, there may come a time when both have changed so much that maintaining their relationship is no longer possible. In this case, maintaining the relationship can cause more harm than breaking it up. It is important to realize that relationships are dynamic and can change over time as our experiences. It is important to respect yourself and your partner and make the decision that is best for you and your relationship.

****

For parents: Your children are not your possessions. They are unique individuals with their own desire for life. At the same time, your children have their own unique personality and their own path in life. You can support them and love them, **but you cannot change their identity or guide them down a path that is not their own.** Either way, you should allow them to express themselves and grow as authentic individuals.

****

If you are afraid to decide which solution to choose, take a pen and paper and answer the following questions maybe this will help you.

What do I want to win?

What do I want to avoid?

What am I willing to risk?

What effects will there be on me and on those involved?

What do others stand to gain and what will they risk?

Analyze each solution if it has everything you want according to what you answered above.

****

When deciding for others you should take care of what is best for the other person and not just look at what is good for you. You have to allow them to choose too, to have a say and not to impose your wishes on them. Example: You are a parent and you choose that your child can eat ice cream now and not when he asked for it. Let it choose the flavor and type of ice cream. Another example: A company manager who has to make a decision to reorganize his business activities must take into account the effects of the changes on his employees and on his customers. In this case, do a gallop- poll to see how your employees and customers see any changes you are thinking of making. Who knows, they might even give you better ideas.

****

When you work on something that you like and that the world or even a part of the people needs, then you will wake up and feel great. Unlike how you fell for the rest of your day when you hate your job. In this case, if for whatever reason you can't find something to do that fills you up, before you go to work and after you come back, make sure you do things you love and that make you laugh.

Don't let your life be spent in sadness. Don't let one activity dictate how you feel every day. Take an hour or half an hour before going to work to laugh by watching at least funny videos. While you are going to the bathroom or on your break again watch funny videos or something that will make you smile. And as you are done working for the day, do something that will relieve you and fill you with optimism. It is not that difficult. It's a matter of habit. Like you used to give in to the nasty feeling of loathing your job letting it take over you all day and the next and the day after that..... Change your bad habits.

****

If you are a boss, praise your employees. It will motivate them.

If you are an employee who longs for praise that never comes, take satisfaction in the fact that you are doing your job well and your customers and colleagues are satisfied with you. Give yourself the credit.

****

Competition should not make us feel less. As long as we do our best that alone should fill us with satisfaction. If there was no competition, no one would try to become even better. If you go running with a friend who runs faster than you, you will end up getting better and better at running. That's how you see the competition. How it helps you to be motivated to try and improve.

****

When you try something once you gain experience. When knowing the consequences you do it again then you are self-destructive. When we don't analyze our experiences and pay attention to them, we will continue to make the same "mistakes".

****

Do your job the best you can and if your boss keeps yelling at you even though you are doing your job right, don't take it personally. Don't take it home and take it out on others. Don't pay attention to him. The unhappiness he feels makes him so. He was not taught to love joy. Try the methods given to you far above to get to the level of not caring.

****

We forget that beyond what we do in our work, in our lives, there are thousands of others who work hard for us so that we, in turn, do what we do. To have electricity, to get to work etc. Let's not forget this and treat our fellow human beings with kindness and gratitude. And they in turn will spread the joy we offered them. This way you will create a great circle of optimism and gratitude!

****

Make the most of the changes life brings you and you will get the best that life has to offer.

****

How can I react to this particular case with compassion and combine my effort to live a better life?

****

We all need help. Today me, tomorrow you. But this need for help does not mean that one is helpless and the other powerful. It's just a temporary situation.

****

A selfish person only cares about himself. He wants to take. He sees the world only in terms of what he can get from it. He lacks concern for the needs of others and respect for their dignity and integrity. He judges everyone and everything according to their usefulness to him.
He doesn't love himself, in fact he hates him. This lack of love and care for himself, makes him feel an emptiness inside. So, he feels frustrated and unhappy. That is why he desperately seeks to grab the satisfaction that he himself prevents himself from enjoying. It may appear that he is overly concerned with himself, but in reality, he is trying to cover up the failure that he feels.

****

The selfless person who wants nothing for himself and lives only for others, may say that he feels proud that he does not consider himself important but he is not happy. And that his relationships with those close to him are not satisfactory. These people feel enmity towards life and are self-centered. They cannot love and enjoy anything.

****

Modern man has distanced himself from himself, his fellow men and nature. He has become a product and perceives his life as an investment that should bring him the maximum profit. Human relationships are meant to keep people thinking the same and not having different thinking, feeling and reacting from others. Even though we're supposed to try to be close to each other for safety, we end up feeling alone. We feel insecure and lonely. Our culture offers many sedatives that help us maintain a conscious ignorance of loneliness and stay in the routine of mechanical work to constantly buy new things to feel satisfied.

****

Most relationships end up as a well-oiled partnership between 2 people who remain strangers throughout their lives and never reach a deep relationship but may try to make each other feel good. It is simply providing a refuge from the helpless feeling of loneliness.

When people live on autopilot without dreams, goals, optimism. Without looking for the joy and meaning of life. When they don't improve. When they live with the fear that society bombards them with, how will they ever learn to love deeply?

****

Where can laziness arise from? It may be the reaction against our routine. Because man is obliged for at least 8 hours a day to spend his energy on purposes that are not his own and in a way that he does not choose, even the pace of work is predetermined, he reacts and this reaction takes this childish form . This discipline that is imposed on him from everywhere and does not leave him time and space to do things that he wants and fills him, fills him with unhappiness and reacts with inactivity.

When we fill our lives with a lot of activities and do many things together we forget how to stay focused, how to stay with ourselves, how to calm down. We become nervous, anxious, tired, lack concentration and seek food, smoke, etc. When we find ourselves alone we don't know what to do.

****

Learning to be alone with yourself and your thoughts even for 1-2-3 hours is very important! It is a condition for being able to love!

****

Learn to concentrate on what you are doing and not listen to TV and talk and do a bunch of other things. Learn to live the moment to the fullest. Otherwise, life passes you by and you don't notice anything. You live on autopilot. You don't pay attention to those you love, nor to yourself.

****

When you feel sad, angry, have some bad feeling, don't give in to it and start thinking bad thoughts. Ask yourself:

What happened;

Why am I angry (what you feel)?

Deal with how you feel. Notice it.

****

When you were little kids what did you love to do? As simple as it seems to you, write it down.

What were you really good at school?

In your childhood, did even one person tell you how good you were at something?

In middle school, high school, did even one person tell you how good you were at something?

What did you say you want to be when you grow up?

What kind of games were the games you played? Which character would you choose?

After school what did you like to do?

Is there something from your childhood that really touched you and you said this is what I want?

Now as an adult what do you love to do in your spare time?

What do you give money to easily?

If you love reading, what kind of books do you prefer?

If you like to cook, what kind of food do you like to make?

Is there a topic of conversation that you always start?

Is there a topic you can talk about for hours?

Any topic you took the time to study on your own?

Look at what you have written, is there any connection between them? Are they all about a specific topic?

 This is yet another way to find out what your life purpose is or else your calling or the profession that suits you.

****

Maybe we do not want to overcome a feeling, a belief because:

Because you've become familiar with it because you've felt it for so long and don't know how to be without it?

Do you think this is how you protect yourself?

Are you afraid that you will lose power or control over others without it?

Are you afraid of losing the attention of others?

Are you afraid of losing your value?

That you will allow others to not feel guilty for what they have done to you?

Are you afraid that without it you will have to take charge of your life?

Are you afraid that you will be happy without it and you fear it because you don't know how? Etc.

In what situations do we question our worth and lose self-love, appreciation and acceptance? Think about it and write your answer.

****

When and in relation to what behavior or personality traits of others do we lose feelings of love, acceptance and unity with others and with ourselves?

****

Write a list of the names of the people you would like to forgive and next to it what they did to you. In this way we stop covering up our pain and give it space to experience it to reduce its intensity.

****

When our value depends on what others think of us, we no longer know who we are. We no longer know what we believe, what we want. We waste our lives trying to be who we think others expect us to be. We become unhappy, bitter from so much oppression. We have not gotten the love and respect we want from others.

****

Another wrong way to measure our value is: My value depends on the success of my efforts for happiness, health, financial comfort, social acceptance, etc.

****

Ask yourself:
Without the others I cannot do (write what).....
Others are responsible for my...........(for what?)
I feel responsible for the following people regarding (their success, health, etc.)......
I expect help from (which people) and to satisfy my needs (what needs?)......
****

Our value cannot be increased or decreased by the behavior of others. We are who we are, regardless of their behavior and their opinion of us.

We have the inner power and wisdom to create our reality towards our evolution. And if, sometimes, we don't have the support of others, that's okay, it's an opportunity for even greater progress.

****

Talk about what's bothering you, say what you think, without blaming, without making them defensive.

Talking without accusations and forced defensive reactions is very important for communication and conflict resolution. When we are bothered by something, it is important to be able to express ourselves respectfully to others. Because we want results.

Examples of how to have a conversation without accusations:

Instead of saying "You're the reason I can't do what I want", we can say "I find it difficult to do what I want because of the circumstances around me".

Instead of saying "You are unfair", we can say "I disagree with your decision".

Instead of saying "I can't stand your behavior," we can say "I'm bothered by some of your actions."

Examples of how to have a conversation without forced defensive reactions:

Instead of saying "I don't know why you always have to do it this way," we can say "Can you explain to me why you prefer to do it this way

Instead of saying "I don't like that you water the flowers every day", we can say "Could we discuss the way we water the flowers to find a better solution?".

Instead of saying "You're useless at your job", we can say "Can we discuss ways to improve your performance at work?".

Instead of saying "You don't know how to cook", we can say "Could we try some new recipes together?".

Instead of saying "I don't believe you", we can say "Can you give me more details or explain how you see it?".

Instead of saying "I don't like your idea", we can say "Could you explain more about why you think this is the best option?".

Instead of saying "I don't understand you", we can say "Can you give me more information or explain how you see it?".

Instead of saying "I don't agree with you", we can say "Can you explain more about your thinking so I can better understand your point?".

****

Some people develop defense mechanisms when we don't feel safe. We close in on ourselves, busy ourselves with some mechanical activity. Others become aggressive, competitive, or compete with others. We grow up in a certain environment and we got different messages about ourselves, about life, about others. Each of us forms a personality with specific and unique needs, desires, habits, beliefs, attachments and what roles we play. Many of our behaviors are defense mechanisms or specific ways of thinking and acting that we hope will protect us from various mostly imaginary dangers.

****

When we have someone close to us who lives **in the position of the victim**, we need to express our love to them, in a way that they can feel it, without getting trapped in feelings of responsibility or guilt. We need to help them find another way to get what they need without self-pity and unnecessary suffering.

The "victim" needs to feel unhappy. He finds daily reasons not to be happy. Others are always to blame for these reasons. It is difficult for them to say "what a wonderful day", "how happy I am", "thank you for being so good to me", etc.

It requires attention and for us to discover the beliefs and feelings we feel when we think about them and when we talk to them. We have to be careful not to get fill with a bunch of negative emotions. Not to be deprived of our energy and our optimism.

We can ask them questions that will help them understand what they need to do to create their own happiness and realize how blessed they are. To encourage them to use their inner strength.

Let's not forget that we are not responsible for their feelings. If they accuse us, with love we tell them that they are wrong and that if they want it, we are here to help them find solutions.

Let's not forget that we are doing the best we can.

Example:

"I want you to know that I care about you, I love you and I want you very much to be well, satisfied and happy. I really want it. However, I am beginning to realize that this is something I cannot create for you. I realize that I feel responsible, even guilty at times, because you are not as fulfilled and happy as we would both like you to be. I understand that feeling this way doesn't help at all. Feeling this way makes me angry with you and I think that you don't try as hard as you could to create your own happiness and you can't see how beautiful life is. This happens, mostly, when you complain about things you don't have, instead of appreciating all that you do have. I will love you and offer you what I can without doing more than I believe and without getting angry with you because you are not satisfied. I will not try to gain your approval and create your happiness. Is there anything you want to share with me about what I just told you?"

****

When we want to make changes, we share them with love without judgment. We explain to them the changes we will try to make and ask for their support. We don't use this knowledge selfishly by telling everyone what role they "play" and categorizing them. This analysis is for us only and we do not use it to hurt and control others.

****

How to deal with someone who always judges you:

"I would like to discuss with you a problem concerning our communication. I feel like I have to apologize for everything I do. You often question and correct me. This forces me to sometimes play the victim and sometimes the terrorist to defend myself. I sometimes act like you.

This way of communicating makes me feel sadness. For this reason, I will try to accept myself, even when you question and criticize me.

I will stop answering your questions and apologizing to your accusations. I will try to be happy with you even when you are not satisfied with me, when you comment and blame me.

Please do not misconstrue what I am saying. I love you; I want you to be happy and live harmoniously together, but we can't be happy like this, with you playing the lawyer and me playing the culprit. I'm not willing to put myself down by playing this game anymore.

I want you to know that I love you, even when I'm not trying to convince you that what I'm doing is right every time. »

****

How to deal with someone who threatens, shouts, terrorizes:

They think others are wrong. They want to punish. To coexist with them when we cannot avoid them, we need to overcome our fear. Let's calmly wait for them to calm down and think about how unhappy this person is. The louder they shout, the more they need compassion. What is this need of them, what fear makes them behave in this way? How can we help them to feel confident and safe with us?

When they calm down, explain to them that although we have no intention of hurting them and making them unhappy, we too have needs and if we don't meet them, we will be unhappy and negative towards them.

We're not going to back down because he-she yells, but we're willing to compromise because we love him- she, as long as he calmly tells us what he wants from us.

Example:

"I need to talk. Sometimes I'm afraid of you. When you yell and threaten me, you awaken in me old fears from my childhood. To avoid conflict with you, I retreat by suppressing my needs and sometimes my values. I lose my self-respect and feel injustice and anger. Then I love you less and sometimes I want to take revenge on you.

The way you act, you may be getting what you want at the moment, but you are losing my love and respect. I decided to try not to be afraid of you and be more honest with you. I will try to express my needs and my values to you, even when you yell or scare me.

Please help me in this endeavor. I am interested in helping you meet your needs. I think we can both have what we want without you threatening me.

I'll tell you my needs, you tell me yours, without threatening me. Without forcing myself to close myself off because I'm afraid of you."

****

What emotions did we feel as a child?

What beliefs about ourselves, about others and life were created in our minds then?

What were our unmet needs at that time?

Has anyone ever gotten angry with us, argued with us, rejected us, or blamed us? Who and when?

Were there people who argued with each other and rejected or hurt each other? Who and when?

Have we ever felt left out?

Did they ever leave us alone somewhere?

Have we ever felt like they are distant and they don't understand us? When; Who; In what way;

Do we need more affection and tenderness? By whom and when and in what periods?

Have we had people often talk about illness or being sick? Who and when?

Did we experience the feeling of humiliation? In what cases?

Have we ever been compared to others? With whom and when and for what abilities or characteristics?

Did we ever hear our parents make love? How did we feel?

Did our parents often tell us that they have sacrificed a lot for us and that we should be indebted to them? Who; For what subjects? What exactly do we owe them?

Did they told you that you are to blame for their unhappiness, illness, problems? Who accused you and for what? What does this mean for you? According to them what should you have done?

Have you been told that you will never do anything in your lives, that you are lazy, incompetent, not smart? Who and for what matter?

Were we often talked about guilt and punishment? Who; When; What kind of guilt and punishment?

At school did the teacher cut you down? By what criteria?

In groups, did you feel rejected or disadvantaged?

They made us understand somehow that in order to be accepted and loved, someone should: be better than others, first in everything he does, perfect, intelligent, beautiful, have many romantic successes, have social and financial success, etc.

As children, we often make wrong conclusions about reality. We consider ourselves responsible for everything, for our parents' anger, failure, abandonment, etc. We conclude that we do not deserve the love, attention, etc. that we need.

 This is why it is so important to learn our behaviors and where they come from and improve them.

****

A few more ways to learn more about yourself and what suits you:

What was most important to you in:

Up to our 9 years?

From 9 to 12?

From 13 to 15?

From 15 to 18?

From 19 to 21?

From 22 to 25?

****

If you were told that you will die in 5 years but until then you will be healthy and active, what would you change in your lives?

In your family?

In your work?

In your personal time?

In your social life?

****

If you make 3 wishes to a genie, what will they be?

****

What talents and abilities do we think we have innately?

****

If everything seems too much from what you've read so far, at least do this: Every time you go to the bathroom for whatever reason start saying to yourself "**I love me, everything is perfect or everything is wonderful or I'm so happy.**" Wait in lines or in traffic start saying it over and over to yourself. Go to sleep, until you fall asleep saying it over and over. You're brushing your teeth, say it to yourself while you're brushing them.
Put it in your everyday life. And you will see how your health and your everyday life will change. At first you will say it and you won't believe it. That does not matter! Keep saying it non-stop!!

****

Say that you really love and respect yourself. What would you do; What would you change?

****

Let's assume that you have changed the way you react and think: After you give up all your excuses, all your victim stories, all the reasons why you cannot and why you have not up until now, and all your blaming of outside circumstances, **if something does not turn out as planned, you have to ask yourself**:

"How did I create that?

What was I thinking?

What were my beliefs?

What did I say or not say?

What did I do or not do to create that result?

How did I get the other person to act that way?

What do I need to do differently next time to get the result I want?

＊＊＊＊＊＊＊＊＊＊＊＊＊＊＊＊＊＊＊＊＊＊＊

In essence, everything we do, our every reaction, affects the events that will happen to us.

Example:

1. If we usually have a negative attitude towards problems, then it is possible that we will also react negatively to future problems, as a result of which we will not be able to solve them in an effective way.

2. If we habitually react with aggression, then it is possible to create a negative atmosphere in relationships and situations that do not require aggression, and this can lead to unpleasant consequences.

3. If we have a habit of procrastinating, then we are likely to find ourselves with tight deadlines and feelings of failure and frustration. This can lead to even more stress and pressure when the deadline for completing tasks approaches and we have to deal with the situation. This may lead to ineffective performance or even failure to fulfill our obligations.

4. If we react in panic to difficult situations, then we may lose our ability to think logically and make effective decisions.

＊＊＊＊＊＊＊＊＊＊＊＊＊＊＊＊＊＊＊＊＊＊＊

When we go to do something and fail there are hundreds of others who have tried and succeeded. So why didn't you make it? Could it be that it has nothing to do with external circumstances since so many others have succeeded? Could it be your thoughts, your beliefs, your habits that have prevented you from succeeding? Are you purposely ignoring useful information and helpful comments from others? Are you thinking negatively, sabotaging your efforts?

Our thoughts, beliefs and habits can significantly affect the results of our efforts and prevent us from achieving our goals. Here are six examples that show how our past thoughts and reactions can influence future events:

1. If one encounters a failure at work and decides that it is impossible to improve, one may not try further, making the failure a belief.

2. A person who has learned to always prioritize work matters may find themselves ignoring their personal needs, affecting their health and well-being.

3. A person who is not used to facing problems may avoid taking on challenges in his life, making himself stay behind others, not moving on.

4. Negative thoughts and beliefs can influence our behavior in the future. For example, if we believe that we are not good at public speaking, then we may avoid opportunities to speak at an assembly or event, thus limiting ourselves.

5. Our past reactions can affect our relationships with other people. For example, if we habitually react aggressively in conflict situations with our fellow human beings, we may alienate friends and associates from us.

6. Our past choices can affect the sense of control we have in our lives. If we constantly make choices that lead to failure or postponement of our goals, we can begin to feel that we are not in control of our lives.

****

The only sure thing in our lives is that we have complete control over three things:

The thoughts we have.

The pictures we make in our mind about how everything is.

How we react. Our actions.

How you use these three determines everything you experience. If you don't like the life you live, you have to change how you use them.

No more negative thoughts. Start thinking positive.

When you relax and dream, change your images. Instead of thinking about what you don't have, what made you angry... see your life in detail having everything you want.

For how you react and act: Change your habits to better ones. Read and listen to other positive things. Change your negative friends to optimistic ones. Change the way you express yourself and speak positively with gratitude instead of being mean, gossipy, angry, etc.

An example of how we cause much, if not all, of what we experience:

Say someone gave you 400 euros. You react by spending them immediately. As a result, you remain the same as before because the joy will go away with whatever you bought. It will not last forever.

Say someone gave you 400 euros. You react by buying a mutual fund or investing them somewhere. As a result, you have an extra passive income. That extra money helps you invest in other ways creating more passive income. And having more money to help others and yourself.

You eat crap and you get fat and sick. **Why** don't you eat better?
You don't say no and they treat you in a way that you hate. **Why?**
You chose the job you are in. **Why?**
You are staying in this job and you don't even look for passive income to be able to leave. Or go learn stuff to be able to evolve, so you can find something better. **Why?**
You constantly ignore your instincts and step on get in to the same trouble. **Why?**
You gave up on your dreams. **Why?**
You made the purchase you now regret. **Why?**
You decided you didn't need anyone's help and now you regret it. It's not their fault that they didn't give it to you, **you** didn't want it. **Why?**
 The thoughts **you** think create your feelings. **You think of them! You chose it! You spoke like that!** *IT IS YOU AND ONLY YOU*!

****

Have you noticed that most of the time we complain to the wrong person? To people who can't do anything about these complaints. They go to work and to their friends and complain about their relationship. They come home and complain about their work. Why; Because it's easier and risk-free. They don't need to take any chances. It is easier than sitting down to discuss it with those involve and try to find solutions.

Those who succeed in their lives react as follows: Instead of complaining, they do! **When they find themselves in a situation, they don't like they try to improve it or leave. They don't just sit there and start complaining here and there**. Nobody owes us anything! If we want something, we have to create it ourselves!

Examples:

1. When a group of friends plans an outing and someone can't attend due to work commitments, instead of declining the invitation, they can suggest organizing a smaller outing the following weekend.

2. When a group of friends goes out to eat and someone is not satisfied with their choice of restaurant, instead of complaining, they can suggest an alternative option and help locate a good restaurant.

3. When a group of friends has planned an activity but bad weather postpones it, instead of canceling the activity altogether, they can suggest it be held indoors or move it for another day or do something else.

4. Communicate openly and honestly with your partner about the problems you face, instead of repressing them and letting them fester.

5. Seek professional help you are facing serious problems in your relationship, instead of ignoring them and hoping they will resolve themselves.

6. Work to improve communication and understanding in your relationship, rather than relying on inadequate and negative attitudes.

7. Acknowledge and respect your partner's or others feelings and needs, instead of ignoring them and insisting on our own opinion and comfortable attitude.

8. Take initiatives to strengthen your relationship, such as suggesting activities that will interest your partner or taking actions that will show your love and interest.

9. An employee who is not satisfied with his working conditions, such as excessive workload or salary, instead of complaining all the time, starts looking for new job opportunities.

10. Two colleagues who disagree about something, instead of seeking confrontation and continuing to disagree, can have a discussion to find a solution and work together better in the future.

11. An employee who does not have the necessary confidence in his own abilities and finds it difficult to take an initiative, can work with a colleague who has more experience or abilities in the specific matter, in order to learn and improve.

12. A boss who does not provide proper education and training to his employees, negatively affects their performance and development at work. Harm both the employees and the business.

13. A boss who is not fair and does not treat his employees with respect and equal treatment can cause frustration and disengagement from their work. Harm both the employees and the business.

14. A boss who doesn't recognize the successes and hard work of his employees can negatively affect their job satisfaction and make them feel undervalued. Harm both the employees and the business.

15. A boss who does not pay enough attention to the health and safety of his employees can cause accidents and injuries and harm both the employees and the business.

16. You didn't attend seminars or classes to improve your skills. You said you don't have time and now a younger kid takes your place or gets paid more than you.

17. You didn't bother to teach your pet or ask a trainer for help and now it's out of control.

18. You didn't put limits on your children, on the people in your life, you didn't follow through on your threats when you said you would cut such and such a privilege if... etc. And now you feel that no one respects you.

 Do you want more or did you get it that it's not others' fault and complaining doesn't get you anywhere?

****

Parents can do a lot to foster a positive mindset in their children. Here are some suggestions:

1. To promote their children's independence: Giving children the opportunity to take responsibility and make age-appropriate decisions can help boost their self-confidence.

2. Focus on effort rather than results: Encouraging their children to do their best instead of focusing on whether they will win or lose can help develop a positive mindset.

3. Show the importance of mistakes: Encouraging their children to try and make mistakes, and teaching them as an opportunity to learn and improve can help develop a coping mindset.

4. To be taught to appreciate and recognize their successes, even in small things, as this increases self-confidence and a positive attitude towards life.

5. Learning to view failures as an opportunity to learn and improve, rather than viewing them as unworthy or a failure.

6. Be encouraged to express their feelings, even if they are negative, and learn to manage them in a constructive way.

7. Teach your kids to learn to recognize the needs and feelings of others, as well as to develop communication and cooperation skills.

8. Instead of allowing your child to complain about difficult lessons, you can reassure them and encourage them to keep trying and improving.

9. Teach your children to take responsibility for their own actions and not place the blame on others.

10. Teach your children the importance of perseverance and discipline and encourage them to keep trying, even when they face setbacks.

11. Teach your children the importance of cooperation and communication so that they learn to work with others and solve problems in a way that benefits everyone.

12. Teach your kids to love and help animals and nature and others. Take them to animal shelters, to a voluntary on cleaning the beach and feeding those in need or something similar.

13. Take them to learn (in seminars or in places to help) about bullying and disable kids. Teach them not to harm others in any way but to be helpful.

****

Let's remember it again! We stop saying:

I feel like I'm the victim in all of this and I didn't deserve it. I feel like he used me. Nothing is wrong. Nothing ever goes right for me. Everything is going wrong for me. Etc.

In place of these expressions, we say:

I'm fine. I feel good. Everything is under control. Everything is fine. Etc.

****

What job and activity would you do for free just because you love doing it? Can you make money by doing it? Or teaching others how to do it? Can you use them to start a blog or a YouTube channel?

****

Let's assume the world is perfect. To be perfect for you what is this world like? How do people communicate? Write in a way that states how this is done. This is your goals!

****

Write 2 of your skills that you consider very important.
Write now in what way you enjoy expressing them.
 If you feel you have more than 2, do these steps for all of them.
Can you make money out of them? Can you teach others and get money? Can you use them to start a blog or a YouTube channel?

****

Make a list of 30 things you want to do now and 30 things you want to do before you die.

****

Now write down 20 things you love, enjoy doing. Look at them and write how you can make money doing them.

****

When a relationship is ended whether is a romantic one or a friendly one or work one, sit and write down the following:
What did this event force you to change in your life?
What did you have to do that you will never do other ways?
What did you learn about yourself?
Did you meet new amazing people?
Did you discover new talents and hobbies of yours?
What positive you gain from being in this relationship?
Don't let this event stay in your heart and mind as one more event that you became a victim! You never were a victim! You started it! You stayed that long!
Start seeing and recording the events from your life in a more positive way than before! Stop creating bad memories and missing the lessons the events wanted you to have!

****

Write: What is your ideal career? Where exactly will you be working? What exactly are you going to do? Who will you work with? What kind of customers should you have? What competitors will you have? How much free time do you want to have? How do you want to spend your free time with friends and family? What hobbies will you have? What kind of vacation are you going to have? How will you have fun? In terms of health, how do you want to be? How do you want your body to be? Your relationships with friends, partners, people around you, clients, how do you want them to be? What car do you want? What house do you want? What will your house be like inside? Where will you live (area)? What kind of neighbors do you want to have? How do you want your finances to be? .... Analyze them in as much detail as you can!

Did you understand where all the above questions are leading you? Those are your goals too!

In learning what you want. How you want it. How to visualize everyday.

****

You magnify something insignificant because you feel the need to be right and everyone else to be wrong.

****

You have to understand that when someone talks bad to you, tells you that you are intolerant, etc. they do it because they just feel angry and bad. **It has nothing to do with you personally**. The same thing happens when they praise you because they feel good. Don't need the acceptance of others!! Don't look for the good opinion of others and don't be scared by their bad opinion!! Know that the problem is not you so don't take it personally!! The opinion others form is based on their own system of thoughts and reality.

****

When someone tells you that what you say hurt them, what actually hurt them is the already existing wounds that your words touched. That is why we say that in essence **we hurt ourselves and others don't hurt us**. We see the world differently and hurt ourselves because we create our own version of events in our minds based on our existing hurts. It all depends on the fear we feel. Without this fear you would not feel anger or sadness.

****

Set it as a reminder to ring frequently throughout the day **"I won't take anything personally"**

****

We make assumptions about what others are doing or thinking and take it personally. Then we blame them and react. We assume something, misunderstand it, take it personally and end up making a huge problem out of nothing!

****

We are afraid to ask for explanations and it is easier for us to make assumptions and we consider them completely correct as if the other person will think like us without having their own personality!

****

When we try to change someone deep down we don't like that person.

****

When you simply do because it fills you and not because you want some reward you will find that you will enjoy what you are doing. Because otherwise you get attached to the reward and start filling up with negative emotions. Give your best and you will receive much more than you expect!

****

staying trapped in the thought that our parents hurt us does not help us to be happy. They taught you what they knew. They did what they could. The fact that they hurt you was the fault of their fears, their own unshakable beliefs and what they were taught. They could not behave otherwise. I'm not saying what they did was right but it's time to move on and be happy!

****

You need to be able to say when you really don't know "**I don't know what to do, I don't know how to do it**"

****

 Listen to what they are telling you and then look inside to see how it makes you feel and ask yourself if it is for your own benefit. Because everything helps us to evolve.

****

It should and **I'm trying** stop saying them! Say **"I create, I do, I intend"**

****

Even anger has its purpose. Notice where that you got angry leads you.
****

When a situation forces you, look at it like this:

Ok, I know there is something here to learn, and something I need to change. **I believe I have the right guidance and I will find what lessons and what positive meanings this situation came to show me.** Without judging, I'll just go with the flow. **I ask that all my changes come with joy, safety and harmony. I experience happiness, security and harmony**.

Then ask this: Why do I have the need to get the attention of others? Don't start "I don't have that need". Yes, we all do. What is missing? Love? Support? What? What came to you came for a reason. Ask those questions and find out why it came.

When something shocks us, it is done so that we stop living and getting caught up in life the way we have been doing it until now and changes must be made.

****

The outside world represents what is happening inside us.

This phrase can be interpreted in several ways.

One interpretation is that our thoughts, sensations, and emotions influence how we perceive and interact with the outside world. If we are negative and depressed, we may see things in a dark way and react negatively. Conversely, if we are positive and optimistic, we can see things in a bright light and react in an open and constructive way.

Another interpretation is that our internal state affects how we cause our experiences. If we are happy and satisfied with ourselves, then our relationships with others and our professional performance can be more successful and satisfying

This proposition means that our internal state, our thoughts, our beliefs and our habits determine how we perceive the world around us and how we interact with it. If we have positive thoughts and beliefs, we will see the world in a more positive light and have more opportunities for success and happiness.

For example, if someone has negative thoughts about themselves and constantly doubts their abilities, then they may face difficulties in finding a job or advancing their career. Conversely, if one has a positive attitude and self-belief, then one can seek and find opportunities for growth and personal success.

Also, if one has a negative attitude towards others and focuses on their negative aspects, then they can distance themselves from their important relationships.

****

If old issues come to mind, they surfaced for a reason. You have to learn something, it is your own treasure. Analyze it. Use the questions in this book

****

When I don't like what's going on maybe it happened to notice something that needs to be change because it really is not working to my advantage and I couldn't see it.

****

Do I feel like a victim? Why?

I feel safe; Why?

What elevates me? Why?

What makes me feel safe? Why?

What does each way of thinking give me? (Negative, positive, aggressive etc. way of thinking. The ones you usually use.)

What do I perceive about myself?

Why didn't I choose to create joy?

Why did I choose to create pain? Or a health problem? Or....

Why did I choose to create this particular health problem?

Am I operating with love?

What makes me feel light?

What does this feeling do for me? (When you feel a negative emotion)

Where does this feeling take me?

****

What are the four decisions that I keep putting off, but if I systematically put them into action, they will change my life for the better? Write!

What are the three steps I can take right now as an example of how I will begin to keep these 4 resolutions?

What pain or negative thought did I attach to my four resolutions to prevent me from carrying them out?

What is the reason or reasons that I don't put them into practice?

Then ask yourself why in each reason you wrote.

What will it cost me now if I don't take action?

What will I gain if I do them?

****

Write 10 reasons why you should change now and why you think you can do it now.

****

What are you thinking about all the time?

In 6 months would you like to.....? and why;

What are the most important things in your life right now? And why;

What traits do you admire and why? (In others & in you)

Would you feel great in your life if there was a what?

What is there in your life that prevents you from being and having what you want? And why;

****

Growing up in the family and environment you grew up in, write down the positives and negatives you got – learn.

What has your life been focused on so far?

Because of what you have lived in so far in your life, what have you been trained-learning by all that? For what purpose? Who you have become because of all that? What habits, believes, characteristics do you have because of how you have lived so far?

What positive intention do you think you are hiding behind the negative events in your life?

What did you get, what did you learn, from your father's behaviors?

What did you get, what did you learn, from your mother's behaviors?

What would you like others to say about you?

What positives do you have?

What would your achievements be?

****

Instead of saying:

You hurt my feelings. You make me feel bad. I can't help but feel that way. You disgust me. Heights scare me. You ridiculed me in public, etc.

Say:

I am hurt because of what I said to myself about your reaction to me.

I make myself feel bad.

I can't help feeling this way, but I have chosen to be angry, to be upset.

I decided to get angry because I can usually impose my anger on others.

I disgust myself.

I convince myself I'm scared of heights.

I'm putting myself in a difficult position.

I oblige myself to feel ridiculous by taking your opinion of me more seriously than the idea I have of myself.

****

You have a 50-50 chance of meeting someone who will disapprove of you when you speak your mind. When someone doesn't approve of what you're saying instead of feeling hurt or changing your mind to gain their approval just see it that you ran into someone from the 50% who would disagree and take it easy. You can say, "**Thank you very much for providing me with more information on this matter.**" If you need to disarm him, say "**I'm going to change my mind now, in order to make you like me, but I actually believe what I said and you should deal with how you feel about all of this.**" (Not liking your opinion)

****

When you find yourself in a boring gathering and you can't avoid it or you cannot make the conversation more interesting, spend your time making plans, writing the first chapter of your book, anything creative for you.

****

Many of our false labels, we put on ourselves to avoid doing something because it was easier for us that way than saying no and backing up our no. And now we have adopted them. Other times because we are afraid to do it- it was easier to use those labels. This is how we perpetuate negative attitudes, phobias, negative beliefs.

Example:

I'm not good at math (a solid excuse to avoid something. I don't make it a goal to get better at math I've found the easy way out).

I'm not good at manual work at all. (Excuse not to do things I don't like because I put the effort to learn how to do only the things I like. This way you reinforce your belief that "I shouldn't deal with things I'm not very good at").

I am shy, nervous, clumsy, disorganized, ugly, forgetful……etc. (you accept and reinforce the label either others had put on you or you put them on you. You don't try to improve. You use it to avoid going somewhere, doing something. You hide behind it).

I'm abrupt, pushy…….(Helps you to keep your hostile behavior. You're not trying to improve. You keep justify your bad behavior).

I'm old, tired……..(excuse for not doing something).

Change it by saying to yourself and others **"Until now I used to act like ……"** or **"Until today I chose to be like this……"** or **"I used to label myself……"** and improve don't hide behind such label's life is wonderful!

End of "this is me" = yes to "this was me or this was how I use to be"

No to "I can't do otherwise this is who I am". Yes to "I can do…..I will try.."

 Finally No to"this is my character" and yes to "that's what I used to think.."

****

Do you think that if you feel guilty enough you will be exonerated of your indecent behavior?

Do you think that if you feel guilty enough you will shift the blame from yourself to others?

Do you think that if you feel guilty enough you will win the pity of others?

Ask yourself what are you avoiding in the present by feeling guilty about the past?

Start writing down when you feel guilty and why – **guilt journal**.

Write down all the bad things you've done. How much guilt do you feel in each and why?

 Evaluate the consequences of your actions.

****

If someone makes you feel guilty, you can react in different ways, depending on the situation and who the person is. Here are some examples of reactions you can use:

1.Ask them to explain why they feel the need to guilt trip you and try to understand their problem.

2.Ignore their challenging behaviors and treat the person with indifference.

3. Ask them if they would like to talk about their feelings and try to help to have a better communication.

4.Tell them that their behavior makes you uncomfortable and ask them to stop.

5.Choose to walk away from the person if you come to the conclusion that they cannot change their behavior and it is not healthy for you to continue being with them.

Here are five examples of situations in which someone tries to frame someone else:

1.A friend who tells you "I'm lonely, I have no one to talk to" when you don't reply to their messages or you do not invite them to your social events. It's important to communicate with this friend in an open and honest way and explain your needs and boundaries without blaming or excluding them.

2. A partner who tells you "You're not taking care of yourself" when you refuse to do something you don't like or that doesn't agree with your values. You can tell him that self-care is important to you and that you don't want to do something you don't like or don't agree with your values just to satisfy your partner's needs.

You can also ask him to support and understand you in your decisions and discuss together how he can help you take care of yourself without undermining your values or your individuality.

3.Coworker who tells you "You're not helping enough" when you don't do their work or do something that isn't your job.

You can **confirm** your co-worker's comment by saying something like, "I understand that you don't think I'm being helpful enough. I'd like to hear more about your perspective."

You can **clarify** your role at work and explain how you contribute to the team's goals. If something is not your job, you can explain this and state your duties.

Collaboration Suggestion: You can suggest working with him more to meet the team's needs. You can discuss who can take on some of the tasks he mentions.

Open Communication: It is important to maintain an open line of communication with your colleagues. You can ask if there are other things you can do to help.

4. A family member who tells you "You don't care about your family" when you don't go to an event or help with the housework.

Explain the reasons why you cannot attend an event or help with household chores. There may be certain necessary obligations that prevent you.

Propose to find a solution that will be acceptable to all. For example, if you can't help around the house at a certain time, you can offer to help at another time, or help by giving instruct the other person to do the work, or offer to help with something else.

Point out that the accusation is unfair and that you take care of your family within your capabilities. (If you really do not lie)

Show your love and care to the family through actions, such as being there when they are needed or helping with family chores more.

5.A friend who tells you "I don't like you anymore" when you don't agree with his opinions or do not do what he wants.

Ask why he feels this way: Your friend may have other reasons that are not necessarily related to what is happening now. Try to discuss the issue and find the real cause of his dissatisfaction.

Explain your point of view: You may not agree with something, but it is important to at least explain your point of view and why you believe what you believe. This may help your friend to better understand your views.

When they answer them don't put words _I think, I believe_. Say "you think and you believe".

Example: your mom goes "You didn't do what I asked. You didn't help me carry......I'll do it myself and let my waist catch me afterwards. Sit and look at your cell phone." You just asked mom to wait a few minutes 2-3 to finish what you are doing. Your response should be, "Okay mom, since you want to do it while your back hurts and you can't wait a few minutes, do it yourself. I guess there's nothing I can do to convince you"

Example: "If you do this I will.......you know very well how much I suffer from........I who sacrificed so many years for you and now you abandon me...." Your answer should be "Do you think that because you helped me when I was a child or ....I have to pay you back for a lifetime, and never become independent..." and just leave.

"You're killing me, that's what you're doing..." Your response "Do you have anything else to say to me before you die?".

****

When you realize that you are anxious about something, ask yourself: What am I trying to avoid right now, using this moment of anxiety?

****

Put a timer on how much you will struggle each day. Say for example 10 minutes in the morning, 10 minutes when I get home, I will think about my worries and then I will go and do various other things that I want and need to do. I will not think negatively and I will also do things to laugh.

****

Write down your worries and after 7 days look at them and ask yourself: Which of your worries have come true? How much did it help you to be anxious for those 7 days about that thing? What is the worst that can happen to you and your family? Compare your answer with what you are struggling with now. What is worse?

****

Go to the mirror and say to yourself "I'm ready to start angsting now". Why do it? To make a little fun of the situation. And reduce its volume.

****

Fear of failure is fear of the unknown. Hang out with lots of different kind of people and you'll see how much you're missing out on and how unfounded many of your fears are.

****

Something more about having extra pounds that torment so many people.

We choose to eat when someone doesn't give us something we want.

We choose not to go out for a walk every day, letting boredom and a bunch of other excuses convince us that it's not our fault that we didn't go out again for one more day.

As long as we don't stop accusing others of not taking care of us, not loving us, etc. we will not make the decision to change our habits and our way of thinking so that can lead us to the result we want.

****

Create your own traditions when you don't want to go to anyone else's.

****

Create your own traditions with your favorite people to add laughter and joy to your days.

****

Write down how many rules you impose on others and why. What does it offer you when others do and when they don't do what you impose on them? How do you feel in each case? How do you feel when you impose things to others? Who taught you this and now you demand it too? How much does it help you and how much does it make your life difficult, acting like that?

****

Make a list of what you hate most about life and yourself and who you blame in each case. That can help you to make your goals too! Your goals are the oppositive! You can even find what to blog about!

****

Better expressions for better communication:

1. You are different from me and even though it is hard for me to admit it……….(and not "would I ever do that to you….")

2. I would prefer…… (rather than "it's not fair.." or "unfortunately...")

3. I would feel better if ……. Example you had called me (and not I always call you…….you never do the same.).

The words **possibly, hopefully, I hope so,** they state that you will not do it and that you prefer inaction. And it's a negative way that shows how little you believe in yourself and your abilities.

I hope everything will be fine = **I'll make sure it's fine**.

I hope everything goes well = **I will do this and that so that everything goes well**.

Everything will probably be fine = **I'll make sure it's fine**.

****

To change complaining and judgmental behaviors you first need to record them each time you do them so you can notice and change them.

****

He who does not act often, judges' others constantly. He has nothing to do and is constantly commenting on the actions of others.

They hurt all the time and blame others for it.

****

Would you act this way if you only had 6 months to live? (Ask yourself this in every problem, in every fear, etc.)

****

If someone tries to judge you, ask them: "Do you think I need your opinion?"

****

Instead of saying "Why don't you treat me well..." ask yourself "**What am I doing so that others can learn to treat me better?**" Nothing?

****

Anger is a choice and a habit. Anger is the result of our wanting the world and people to be different. It is the reaction to disappointment.

****

Mistakenly thinking that anger, irritation is something spontaneous does not help you in anything. **You're just justifying your bad behavior.** Because you don't want to bother improving it. Think like that: "Things are not going the way I wanted them to. Even though I don't like it, I'm not going to get angry, I'm not going to get upset." "Because I get angry and outraged, I urge others involved to choose unhappiness."

"He makes me angry or he gets on my nerves", clearly states that the other person's behavior makes you unhappy.

"Crush the opponents or crush him" is not a simple expression, it is encouragement and **legitimization of violence and anger.**

Every time you get angry think that the other person has the right to be different, to think differently, to react differently, etc.

****

Just be content with "Ok, we are different and we don't have to agree on everything" and then move on, have a conversation, do something to laugh.

****

Expressions of someone who is victimized. He lets others manipulate him out of fear, out of insecurity, because it suits him, so he has someone else to blame.

But he promised me he would...

I knew I shouldn't let him handle it........

It meant so much to me... I knew that I shouldn't trust her since she doesn't care.........

They fooled me again.................

I'll show them, they can't do that to me...

When will I learn............

I hope he doesn't get mad at me.......

He'll surely think I'm a fool...

Would you mind if I ask something........

I beg you, pleaseeeee is it possible.......

Stop expressing yourself in such a way that shows others that you are becoming a victim. When you know that the person you are going to meet belittles you or talks down to you or in any way makes you feel and act like a victim, don't go or prepare what you will say and how you will handle the situation. Don't go with the "I know I'm going to lose" or "I get upset every time..." mentality.

If others find out that you are afraid to face challenges, they will brutally impose on you. If you think you are a victim, you will become a victim.

So, ask yourself:

What do I gain by being a victim?

Why do I find it easier to be a victim than to stand up for myself?

Maybe so I don't become a target?

Maybe to avoid any risks and responsibilities?

Maybe so I don't have to make decisions?

Maybe so they don't blame me later if something goes wrong?

Maybe to collect the credit and rewards without doing anything?

Victimizing expression = non-Victimizing:

Why did you do it like that? = what did you learn by doing this like that?

If you had asked me from the beginning….. = it will be better in the future to consult me first.

But that's how we've always done it! = You are different now; you want different things and I find it difficult to accept that.

 If I hadn't done this now….. = I see where things went wrong and I will never make the same mistake again.

$$* *$$

When you argue with someone your argument reinforces his lack of understanding and helps him stick to his point of view more. **Arguing just reinforces the point he has and how strongly he wants to push it.** If you allow yourself to be dragged into an argument thinking that you will succeed in making the other person understand you, you will end up the victim. **Even if you win you will have lost because you will feel upset, tension, a lot of negative emotions.**

$$* *$$

When you try to prove your worth to others you are declaring that you need something like that and you will always be under their control.

****

Learn to apologize and get up and leave. Even when you are in a public place with others. Change your habit of suffering in silence.

****

Name the other person's feelings when they are about to start a fight or when they are angry. Example: "**You feel really bad**, about this and... to make me feel bad too." "**You don't understand** me and **you're angry** because I let you down." "**You hurt yourself**...". "I decided not to fight about it. If you persist, you will fight yourself. Either we will discuss calmly, with respect for each other, or I will not participate at all." **Show that you understand the other person's feelings and you are not afraid to reveal them**.

****

Complaining that, for example, your wife is a closed person and it bothers you that she doesn't talk to you more. What do you expect from a closed person? You get annoyed because she does something completely expected. Example 2: Worrying that your child doesn't like soccer and labeling him as not for sports, what do you expect? How can you expect him to be good at something he doesn't like? Who's the crazy one here? The child who does something expected or you who wants him to love football even if he hates it? Could you love something when you hate it or when it is not how you behave?

****

Eliminate violence from within so that when you react, you don't get angry and sad because someone doesn't see the world the way you do.

****

Get rid of this obsessive thought that because someone is in your life (partner, child, friends, colleagues, etc.) they owe you something.

****

Live and face life: How can I turn it into an amazing experience? What can I say, feel or do to bring me learning and fulfillment? Start enjoying everything you come across on your way.

****

Epilogue

I could go on write and write more pages but I don't want too over do it. If you want more go to my blog and to my YouTube and read and see more!

****

If you feel the need to have a group where you can talk about your goals without being joke about.

If you feel the need to have a group where you can share your problem to help you see the positive in the whole situation and why not, maybe, someone can help you practically…….

Let's create it! Join my group at **Facebook** https://www.facebook.com/groups/2666616056803470/

****

If what you read really helped you and you want to support me in my endeavors (writing this book, making videos, writing on my blog and more) subscribe to my social media, my web page………(.below are all the necessary links on how you could support me if you want) And I will be very happy if you tell me what helped you from what is in the book and how it changed your life for the better! And what do you think is missing and what you did not like!

****

For Donation: PayPal email: ddoitbetter@gmail.com

Tiktok: https://www.tiktok.com/@kalliopiziplon

Instagram: https://www.instagram.com/do.it.better.kalliopi/

Web page: https://amazingcreationsshop.wixsite.com/life-is-amazing

YouTube: https://www.youtube.com/@youcandoitbetter

Discord group: https://discord.gg/SPkS4zZ7yn

****

If you need help finding an idea to start a YouTube channel or how to turn your "pain" into a YouTube channel and more... and make a blog and a Facebook page and put your texts and videos there too, I can help you.

How much would you pay for? I am happy to discuss pricing options with you to ensure that you receive quality feedback at a fair rate

1. Offer one: which is to give you a document either in pdf format or in notebook format, where inside it will be the tools you will to get started on your own. Links with tools on how to make a video, how to do this and that in a freeway. Questions that by answering them you will find the idea to create your channel. Tips from my own experience…..
2. Offer two: All of the above and if you are still struggling, we can talk in writing about how to find your idea and the advice you would receive.

****

Are you in need of someone to test the user-friendliness and ease of navigation of your blog or webpage, and provide feedback on its readability and searchability? If so, I can assist you in this matter.

How much would you pay someone to do this for you? I am happy to discuss pricing options with you to ensure that you receive quality feedback at a fair rate.

****

Are you looking for someone who can transform your text or ideas into engaging and humorous poll questions and answers, which you can use to gather feedback from your audience, customers, or partners via social media or via a poll? Or just make your people react in your social by poll. Or do you want to know the changes you have done or the ones you are planning on doing how your audience, customers, or partners feels about them by doing a poll? If so, I am here to assist you.

I would be delighted to discuss pricing options with you and ensure that you receive top-quality work at a fair rate. With my expertise in creating engaging and entertaining poll questions, I can help you generate valuable feedback in a fun and creative way.

How much would you pay someone to do this for you and for how many questions?

****

Are you writing a book and want someone to read it and give you their opinion? I can do it!

How much would you pay someone to do this for you? Depending of course and how many pages it is.

****

You don't have the money yet to pay someone very specialized (with degrees at that) to write your life story in a book or texts to post or to translate something for you from English to Greek and vice versa? I can help you.

How much would you pay someone to do this for you depending of course and how many pages it is?

Don't forget that if you want me to help you write your book, your idea is in your amazing mind and you will need to share it with me somehow. By giving me your notes? By what way?

****

Do you want someone to send you daily encouraging little messages to your email depending on the difficulty you are going through so that you don't forget to think positively? Or to remind you of your goal so you don't give up? I can help you.

How much would you pay someone to do this for you?

****

You wrote a book and you can't make a cover yourself, you don't want to deal with it, you have no ideas and you can't pay too much to have it done for you……. I can help you.

Here you can see a small sample of covers I made: https://youtu.be/VM_bq_cn3eo

 How much would you pay someone to do this for you and how many demos?

****

If you are interested in any of the above contact me and write me exactly what you want (how many pages or questions or…) and how much you pay for it.

<u>Payments are made via PayPal</u>.

****

Sources

Let me make it clear that I am not being paid by anyone to show you, their links. I'm just sharing with you the research I did. I do this to save you the trouble of doing all this research yourself. The purpose of this book is to help you!

****

Because I didn't have it in my mind back then that I would write this book, I didn't kept all the links from the many wonderful seminars I attended thinking - since I'm on their list when they will do again another free seminar they will inform me... and some of their links expire after the seminars are done…..
So, I am putting you their Facebook groups if you want to ask to join to watch when they are doing a free seminar again and maybe they may have the videos of their past seminars.

****

1.A positive way of thinking (by Positive mindArt):
2.https://www.facebook.com/groups/4762301347219668/
3.Harmony Coaching Ομάδα:
https://www.facebook.com/groups/528862460958227/
4.Dean Graziosi = https://www.youtube.com/c/deangraziosi the man has incredible energy and his videos cheer you up a lot, motivate you! He did an amazing seminar, free, Dean Grazios 2023 New World Blueprint Strategy Session.
5.Tony Robbins: He has a bunch of books on goals and how to achieve them. And he did a great free Become Unshakeable Challenge tutorial. See the videos he uploads here = https://www.youtube.com/channel/UCJLMboBYME_CLEfwsdul0wQ

6.Dr Joe Vitale: He has a great offer for 3 dollars that gives you a great book and many useful videos from his lectures and in it is the technique of how to erase your negative beliefs! Of course, I took the offer! https://www.joevitale.com/zero-limits-living-tv & https://www.youtube.com/@JoeMrFire

Another nice seminar for free was this one too =
7.https://www.myneurogym.com/brainathon/brain-retraining/?first=%CE%9A%CE%B1%CE%BB%CE%BB%CE%B9%CE%BF%CF%80%CE%B7&last=%CE%9A%CE%B1%CF%80%CE%BB%CE%B1%CE%BD%CE%B9%CE%B4%CE%BF%CF%85&hemail=life.is.amazing.ziplon@gmail.com&contactId=&bm_id=39f81c11627c&utm_medium=cp&utm_source=em&utm_campaign=wtgm_bwt&utm_content=dts-09-v01&el=cp-em-brain_wealth-dts-09-v01&engagement_action=emcp-wtgm-se&mkt_tok=NTE5LVZPVy04MTIAAAGJ5-cPfgscYCFN2L8HOpqXtcZKbaSvyq3E0V5ZQOuJoOl8_tYmsslsDLmp7NfU2m6XOQ5UMYaUQTp-uSgukWEED0Q02BoqZ_pNhuV8eZec

8.**Michelle Kopper :**https://michellekopper.com/
And the group at Facebook =
9.https://www.facebook.com/groups/PowerUpYourPresence/posts/2322872964544395/?utm_medium=email&utm_campaign=1567882-free-training-12-days-of-visibility-day&utm_source=lists%2F153426-Opt-In-Giveaway-Heart-of-Coaching-Jan&simplero_object_id=su_8wvdJTW5h7uLDJiwQ8KEPmoy
10.Rich German: https://www.getjvreadynow.com/misc-5539577316577483800668
11.Jeff Walker: https://jeffwalker.com/why-its-bad-to-wait/

12.Sai Blackbyrn:
https://dashboard.coachfoundation.com/login/?inf_contact_key=dabdfa9ba917948f9c78f41c1d1b82b416358d5485884e2f31e6019a0d26c8b0

13.Hay House: https://www.hayhouse.com/
14.Melinda and Omar Martin: https://higherlevelstrategies.com/

15. One more: marketing@invitechange.com

16.Become Unshakeable 2023 Challenge: Official Tony Robbins Community =
https://www.facebook.com/groups/tonyrobbinscomebackchallenge/

17.Coaching Community:
https://www.facebook.com/groups/coachingfoundationcommunity/

18.Coach & Grow R.I.C.H. (Rewarded. Inspired. Confident. Happy.) Community:
https://www.facebook.com/groups/CoachAndGrowRichCommunity/

19.Global Heart Healing Community:
https://www.facebook.com/groups/globalhearthealing/

20.Transformational Leadership Cafe: Master The Art & Skill of Guiding Others:
https://www.facebook.com/groups/5941197174082411/

21.The Neuroscience of Goal Achievement:
https://www.facebook.com/groups/brainathon/

22.Virtual Coach Community:
https://www.facebook.com/groups/virtualcoachcommunity/

23.DrJoeVitaleZeroLimits: https://www.facebook.com/groups/drjoevitalezerolimits/

24.Hay House 4-Day Book Writing Challenge October 2022:
https://www.facebook.com/groups/hayhousebookwritingchallengeoct2022/

25.Global Heart Healing Community =
https://www.facebook.com/groups/globalhearthealing

****

Books:

Of the few books I have kept…. because I had filled them with underlines and they were not accepted in the library that's why I still have them hahaahahha. Amazing books. Maybe some of my notes are from them. They are worth reading!!! I have them in Greek. I translated the titles hoping they are as close as to the real ones.

1. The Power of self-healing or The Essence of Self-Healing: How to Bring Health and Happiness into Your Life – Petrene Soames

2. Plato, not Prozac! The application of philosophy to everyday problems. – Lou Marinov.
3. The art of love or the art of loving – Erich Fromm
4.Energy Psychology for freedom from fear and every obstacle to health, peace, happiness and the realization of your goals. – Robert Ilias Najemy. (Maybe it is for free like many others he gives away)
5. Take 100% responsibility for your life. Jim Rohn.
6. The Four Agreements – DON MIGUEL RUIZ
7. Your Fault Areas – WAYNE DYER
8. To move your own strings - WAYNE DYER

****

Thank you for reading my book!
Your feedback is most welcome!
I wanted to make this eBook more good-looking but the platforms that allow to self-publish don't allow that kind of files.
That's why I am leaving it be simple as it is.